The World
of Young
Tom Jefferson

Suzanne Hilton

illustrated by William Sauts Bock

Walker and Company
New York

First published in the United States of America in 1986 by the Walker Publishing Company, Inc.

Published simultaneously in Canada by John Wiley & Sons Canada, Limited, Rexdale, Ontario.

Book design by Irwin Wolf

Library of Congress Cataloging-in-Publication Data

Hilton, Suzanne
   The world of young Tom Jefferson

   Includes index.
   Summary: Describes the childhood and youth of Thomas Jefferson in the context of the eighteenth-century Virginia society in which he lived.
   1. Jefferson, Thomas, 1743-1826—Childhood and youth—Juvenile litera-ture. 2. Presidents—United States—Biography—Juvenile literature.
[1.Jefferson, Thomas,1743-1826—Childhood and youth. 2. Presidents.
3. United States—History—Colonial period, ca. 1600-1775] I. Bock, William Sauts, 1939-   ill. II. Title.
E332.27.H55 1986   973.4'6'0924   [B]   [92]   85-29548

ISBN. 0-8027-6621-8
ISBN. 0-8027-6622-6 (lib. bdg.)

Printed in the United States of America
10 9 8 7 6 5 4 3 2 1

CONTENTS

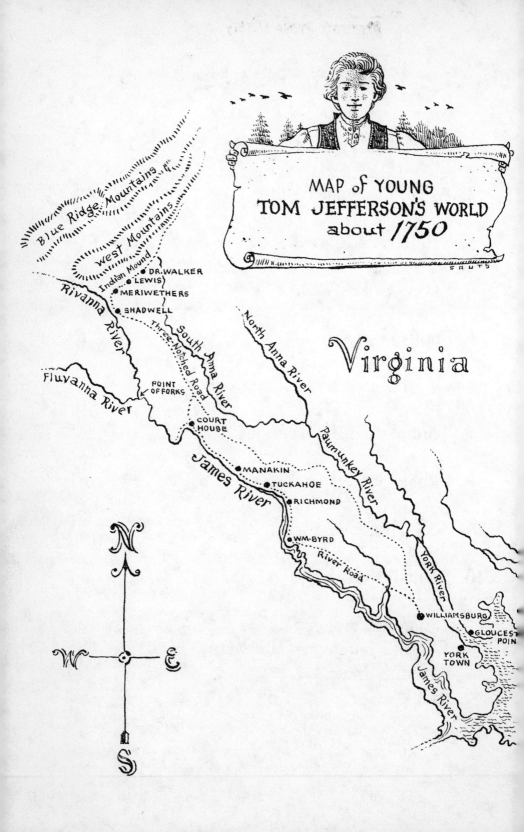

MAP of YOUNG
TOM JEFFERSON'S WORLD
about 1750

SAUTS

Blue Ridge Mountains

West Mountains

Indian Mound

DR. WALKER

LEWIS

MERIWETHERS

SHADWELL

Rivanna River

Three-Notched Road

South Anna River

North Anna River

Virginia

Fluvanna River

POINT OF FORKS

COURT HOUSE

James River

MANAKIN

TUCKAHOE

RICHMOND

Pamunkey River

WM. BYRD

River Road

York River

WILLIAMSBURG

GLOUCEST POIN

YORK TOWN

James River

N

W E

S

1

Up the Three-Notched Road

On April 2, 1743, at Shadwell, Virginia, Peter Jefferson lifted his newborn son Thomas tenderly from his wife's arms. He could not resist carrying him to the front door. After bending down to show the baby to big sisters Jane and Mary, he walked slowly down the wide hallway.

"Shade his eyes," Jenny Jefferson called from the bedroom.

"It's dull outside," Peter soothed his wife. "I just want him to see the plantation he'll own some day."

Several of the slaves had found work to do near the house, in the hopes of seeing the new baby. The master was not the only one pleased that a son had been born. To the slaves owned by Peter Jefferson, a son meant a kind of security for them too. Shadwell plantation would now stay in the Jefferson family instead of being split up among the husbands of Peter's daughters. Dividing land meant a painful dividing of slave families.

Later that night, listening to the slaves celebrate the birth of his son, Peter Jefferson wrote a quick letter to the best friend he had in the world, William Randolph. Without Randolph, there would have been no Shadwell.

Jefferson smiled a little, remembering how embarrassed he had been that night just two years before. He had ridden into Williamsburg wearing an old deerskin jacket, completely forgetting that it was the public times when court was in session. The city was filled with well-dressed planters from all over Virginia. He

brushed a speck of road dust from his jacket and sat taller in his saddle.

That evening Williamsburg seemed packed with people who knew him. At the arsenal were several militiamen he recognized. On Duke of Gloucester Street there were more than the ordinary number of family coaches. Many held friends and even relatives. Some carriages were taking men and women dressed in satins and velvets in the direction of the governor's home.

Peter Jefferson knew that many of the men sporting new blond bob wigs or grizzled brigadier wigs were in the capitol hoping to land soft government jobs. But he took a dim view of Virginians who judged a man more by his outside than by what was under his wig.

Jefferson swung easily off his mare and handed her reins to the hostler's boy at the Raleigh Tavern.

"No feed," he warned. "Just water, and rub her down."

The stable yard was already filled with horses. Williamsburg was always crowded at the public times. The justices rode in from their plantations and held court. The burgesses came from every county in Virginia for the meeting of the legislature. Plantation owners came into town to do business while all these important people were there.

This fourteenth year of the reign of King George II had been a busy one for Jefferson and his wife. Peter had been married to Jane Randolph—his "Jenny"—for almost three years, and he hoped to make this year of 1741 very special for them.

"Evening, Henry," he said to Henry Wetherburn, who was now running the Raleigh Tavern.

"Mr. Randolph's already waiting for you, sir." The innkeeper waved him toward a table.

From Jefferson's lively step, everyone in the room could tell that this was a happy man. In fact his excitement bubbled over even before he sat down opposite his best friend, William Randolph. As Randolph smiled a welcome, Peter Jefferson poured out his news.

"William, I've decided to buy that mountain land we were talking about—the thousand acres plus the four hundred acres along the Rivanna River."

Randolph caught his breath. Jefferson took no notice and rushed on.

"You know that Jenny is soon to have our second child; our baby Jane is almost two now. If this baby should be a son, I want a good plantation for him to grow up on. And a piece of land he can inherit."

"I thought Cousin Jane didn't want to live so far away from Tidewater country," said Randolph.

"We talked it over, and Jenny—that is, your cousin Jane—has already thought of a name for it: Shadwell. That's a favorite place of hers in England. I plan to start by raising a little tobacco and corn, maybe some wheat, set up a mill. . . ."

Something in William Randolph's face made Peter Jefferson slow down.

"Is anything wrong?"

"Peter, I made settlement on that Rivanna River land only two days ago," Randolph admitted.

"You bought it?"

"Did you really want it so very much?" his friend asked. "It's so far upcounty. Way over a hundred miles from Williamsburg, and seventy from my place at Tuckahoe. And you know the law—you have to build a house and plant three acres for every fifty acres you buy. You have so few slaves that you would have to live there yourself to claim the land is seated."

"It's a great piece of land," said Jefferson sadly. "I'm glad it's yours and not some stranger's, anyway."

Randolph was quiet only a moment. Then his face brightened.

"I'll make the deed over to you tomorrow," he said suddenly. "But it's going to cost you something."

Jefferson smiled warily. "How much?"

Randolph let him worry a second before he said, "The largest bowl of Henry's best arrack punch."

Jefferson was overwhelmed. Shadwell—and the deep water along the Rivanna—was to be his and Jenny's. No man ever had such a good friend!

"But what can I do for you?" he asked Randolph.

Perhaps it was Henry's arrack punch with its oriental flavoring, or perhaps a dream had shaken up Randolph a few nights before, but Jefferson could see that something worried his friend.

"I've been wanting to ask you something for a long time." Randolph spoke slowly, his serious eyes looking straight into Jefferson's. "If anything should ever happen to me, would you help my wife raise our children? May I name you an executor in my will?"

Peter Jefferson was not surprised that William Randolph was writing his will. Death came so quickly these days that no man could be sure of seeing the sun rise. If William was sailing to England or going into the wilderness, either was a good reason for making a will. Jefferson told his friend that he was honored to be asked.

As Randolph ladled out more of the arrack punch, he certainly looked like the healthiest man in Virginia. Surely it would seem that he had no need for concern about raising his young children. . . .

A sharp cry from his own newborn son startled Peter back to the present. I have provided for that tiny being, Peter thought, by building this plantation in the foothills of the mountains.

Virginians were split between those people who lived in the Tidewater section and those who moved into the Piedmont at the foot of the Blue Ridge Mountains. Tidewater Virginia is the low land near the large rivers that are swept twice a day by tidal currents.

Peter Jefferson had grown up in Tidewater country near the James River. But the best lands there had been bought up years before by wealthier families than his. Peter's older brother had inherited the plantation of their father. Since Peter was a younger son, he had to make his own fortune. During his years of surveying in the mountains of western Virginia, he had decided that the area at the foot of the mountains was the place where he wanted to raise his family.

William Randolph turned the deed for the Rivanna River land over to Jefferson on March 16, just before the new year began. (The English and people of the colonies began the new year on March 25.) A few days later the Jefferson wagon drivers thumped and lurched over the rocks and tree stumps that littered the only road to the new plantation. April rains had left holes in the thick red clay so deep that the wagon wheels sank down out of sight. Sometimes three yoke of oxen had to be hitched to one disabled wagon to pull it out.

This was called the Three-Notched Road, because the trees marking its route were hacked with three notches. The Three-Notched Road was cleared only a few miles beyond Shadwell, where it turned north toward the Southwest Mountains. A traveler leaving Williamsburg followed either the Three-Notched Road or the River Road, which ran along the north bank of the James River. The River Road narrowed down to no more than an Indian trail long before it came anywhere close to Shadwell.

As soon as they arrived at Shadwell, Peter busied his slaves in putting up a "quick" fence to keep the horses and oxen from wandering off into the hills. They pounded chestnut stakes into the ground every two feet in a straight row, then twisted in boughs from the red cedar trees. Later they would put up a more solid Virginia worm fence with zigzagging bars.

The clear, cool air and the blue mountains came as a surprise to most of the slaves, who had been raised in the low Tidewater country at Peter's father's home. In these mountains, a slave would be able to live in freedom—if he could make friends with the Indians. Few white men would dare chase a slave very far into that wild land. It was a comforting thought as the slaves struggled to clear the land for Peter's house. Later they discovered their master knew the wild land and the Indians who lived there as well as he knew the Tidewater country.

In Virginia no man could keep land unless he used it. If he did not build a house and plant the land within three years, any other man could go to court and claim that land for his own. The reason for this law was that many men received land by patent at a cheap price. Then three years later, just before the patent ran out, they sold the land for three or four times what they had paid for it. Peter Jefferson knew a man named Charles Lynch who bought 400 acres of land for 8 pounds sterling and sold it for 40 pounds two years later.

The governor of Virginia was not interested in making men wealthy. He wanted settlers to live on the land and build towns and forts. The Virginians in the low tidelands were worried about having a war with France. The French had already stirred up the Indians against the settlers in Carolina. If enough pioneers built their homes near the gaps in the westward mountains, the Indians might be kept from attacking the Virginians the way they had massacred the Carolina settlers when Peter Jefferson was a little boy.

Most wealthy planters buying "upper county" land sent an overseer with slaves to establish quarters there. The slaves planted a crop and built crude shelters to live in. The overseer kept in touch with the master by sending riders with news. The planters visited the land, but they rarely moved their families there to live.

Virginia was beginning to fill up with immigrants. Many Scots came down the road from the north to live in the mountains near Shadwell. In the valley on the other side of the Blue Ridge, Germans had built small, neat farms. They had traveled down an Indian trail known as the Great Warrior's Path and widened it so much that it was now called the Great Waggon Road. Neither Scots nor Germans were considered citizens, so they could not vote, even though they had to pay taxes.

Peter Jefferson had made many Indian friends during his surveying trips into the mountains. He felt safe at Shadwell and told Jenny that the location of their new home would not be called "the frontier" or "the upper county" much longer.

"Several of the planters around here think we should form ourselves into a new county. That means building a town nearby to put the county courthouse in. And that will mean new roads, too," he promised.

Jenny Jefferson moved to Shadwell with their daughter Jane sometime after the new baby, a little girl named Mary, was born. By summer Jefferson had his new mill working along the Rivanna River. As he had hoped, the water was deep enough for people to come upstream to the mill in shallow boats.

His wife had a new project of her own to announce. "Our next baby will be born at Shadwell come spring," she told Peter.

"This baby will be our son." Peter hugged his wife, but then he hurried to add, "Of course, I don't mind if it's a daughter."

According to English law, daughters could not inherit land and keep it for themselves. Land belonged to their husbands, and a husband could do whatever he chose with land left to his wife. A man who loved his plantation as Peter did wanted very badly to have a son to inherit it.

That summer a rider from Tuckahoe came to Shadwell to see Mr. Jefferson. William Randolph's wife was dead. Jefferson left at once for her funeral and to comfort his friend. As he was getting ready to return home, Randolph pulled him into a small room and closed the door.

"My friend, if I should die, will you and my cousin Jane come with your children and live for a while at Tuckahoe? I want my children to grow up in their own home and to be a part of your loving family."

Peter agreed at once. The two men talked long about the Randolph children and what education William wanted for his daughters, as well as for his son, Thomas Mann Randolph.

"No school in England," said William. "I've heard of too many children spending unhappy years among strangers. I want him exposed to you, Peter, and to the things you believe in."

Riding back home, Jefferson had to remind himself of his many blessings before he could become his cheerful self again. But thoughts of his Jenny, their little girls Jane and Mary, and of the baby soon to come put a smile on his face.

2

A Very Special Redhead

THE new baby at Shadwell was named Thomas for his grandfather. Captain Thomas Jefferson, Peter's father, had died many years before. The baby's great-grandfather, another Thomas Jefferson, had come to the Virginia colony in 1619 and survived the great Indian Massacre of 1622. Perhaps also, Peter had wanted to name his first son Thomas for his own big brother, whom he had adored. That Thomas Jefferson had died on board the ship *Williamsburg* exactly twenty years earlier. The *Williamsburg*'s captain was the baby's other grandfather, Jenny's father, Captain Isham Randolph.

Whichever Thomas the baby was named for, Jenny knew that their son was going to be special. He was not given those solemn hazel gray eyes and a head covered with red fuzz for nothing.

"Thomas should be christened," said his mother one spring day. "But where? There is no church here, and we hardly ever see a parson."

The nearest church building to Shadwell was the Mountain Chapel on the Three-Notched Road. William Randolph had built it on his land. But since his family had never moved to Randolph's Piedmont plantation, it had no parson, and no regular church service had ever been held in it. Jenny remembered her own christening place in Shadwell, England, and decided the Mountain Chapel was not the place for Tom's christening.

Almost all Virginians attended the Anglican church, just as they would in England. Each man over sixteen belonged to a parish and owed it a percentage of his earnings for the year in church taxes. He was fined or sent to prison if he did not pay. The Jeffersons paid church taxes, even though there was no church near Shadwell to attend. The few English Quakers, Scottish Presbyterians, and German Lutherans who lived in Virginia also had to pay taxes to support the English church. They argued angrily that paying for a state church was one reason they had left their homes in Europe.

A man was in trouble if he missed going to church more than four Sundays in a row, unless he could prove he was sick or had gone to another church one of those Sundays. Or unless, as in the case of the Jeffersons, there was no church to go to. The Bishop of London had ordered each parish to build a church and furnish it with everything needed to hold services. But he could not find enough parsons who would leave England to preach in the colonies.

Sunday had its special laws. A person was fined five shillings for doing any "worldly" labor on a Sunday. Even slaveowners got in trouble for forcing their slaves to work on that day. They argued that it was the custom to go to church and invite their friends back to dinner. How could they invite them to a meal unless their slaves worked?

Anyone caught selling goods on a Sunday was forced to pay a fine and hand over the goods to the poor. The only items that were allowed to be sold on Sunday, morning or evening, were milk and mackerel, because they could not be kept fresh until the next day. The church fined everyone for swearing. A laborer, servant, or common soldier paid one shilling to the poor for each swearword. A swearword from the mouth of a gentleman was worth two shillings.

No record has been found to show how Jenny succeeded in having Thomas Jefferson christened. But since it was an important event for a Church of England member, she must have found a traveling parson to do it.

Baby Tom was born just in time for the tobacco planting. Tobacco was the most important money crop that his father and other Virginians planted. The best kind of tobacco was called simply "Virginny" in England, without even adding the word tobacco. The planters used it for money. A hunter in the Piedmont received one hundred pounds of tobacco for killing a large wolf. Jefferson paid his militiamen in tobacco—fifteen pounds a day to each or-

dinary soldier. Parsons and other churchmen were paid sixteen thousand pounds of tobacco a year. They sent the tobacco to England and received in exchange clothes and furniture.

During the first rains after young Tom was born, Jefferson's slaves transplanted the young tobacco seedlings into the fields. For six weeks every outdoor slave worked to trim the lower leaves and pick off the worms. When the tobacco leaves turned brownish, the slaves cut down the plants and hung the leaves to dry in the tobacco house.

Like all slaves on tobacco plantations, Jefferson's people packed the leaves into large barrels called hogsheads. Hogsheads were rounded and made of wood so tough they could be hitched behind horses and rolled down the road to a warehouse on the river. Most of the roads around Shadwell were "rolling roads" that had been rolled flat by hogsheads of tobacco.

The Jefferson tobacco floated down the Rivanna River into the James River in hogsheads stacked in two canoes lashed together. Below the "falls line," where rapids and falls made it impossible for ocean sailing ships to go farther upstream, the tobacco was stored in a "rolling house" until it was loaded onto a ship bound for England. The ship captain paid Peter for his crop before leaving Virginia.

Most Virginia men did not smoke the tobacco themselves. But smoking was very fashionable in England. Many Virginia fathers refused to send their sons to school in England for fear they would learn to smoke there. Another reason tobacco was popular in England was that a doctor had said smoking prevented the plague, the most dreaded disease in the world. England had not had a plague for fifty years, said the doctor, because the thousands of people who now smoked had caused clouds of pollution over London, and those clouds kept out the plague.

No pollution clouds or plagues hung over Virginia. However, Peter Jefferson felt that the people who lived in some areas were in danger of getting a sickness called the pestilence from the fogs or miasmas that hung over the rivers. Some people blamed the fevers on ships that came from tropical islands. They anchored in the rivers and sick sailors spread diseases on shore. No one even dreamed that the pesky little "moschetoes" could cause sickness in the wetlands.

Three children now lived at Shadwell. The house was one and a half stories high, with space in the garret chambers for bedrooms. The front door opened onto a wide hallway, with another door at the opposite end to attract cool breezes during the hot summer. The four large rooms that opened off the hall were probably the dining room, the withdrawing room, a study, and the parents' bedroom. Each had its own fireplace with the stone chimneys that marked all Piedmont homes.

The windows—the Jeffersons called them "wind-doors"—were just large enough to let in light but not too much cold wind in winter. Peter had grown up in a home with no glass in the bedroom windows. Probably Shadwell did not have glass upstairs at first either. Instead, the windows were covered by shutters that allowed in some light and kept out rain. The closed shutters kept the bedrooms refreshingly cool in summer.

As in most Southern homes, the kitchen was reached by going outdoors, to a separate small building. This kept the cooking noises and smells out of the main house and protected it from burning down, because fires were more likely to start in the kitchen than in any other room. When the meal was ready, slaves carried it into the main house.

Thomas Jefferson always remembered how much he had hated eating cold potatoes and vegetables at Shadwell in winter. Years later, when he built his own home, Monticello, he designed a covered walkway so that his slaves could carry his meals from the outside kitchen up a back stairway to the dining room. That way hot food reached the table in winter still hot.

Shadwell had a cold room under the house to keep apples and potatoes. A springhouse built down into the ground with a cool spring running through it kept eggs, milk, and butter from spoiling in the hot Virginia summers. A cow provided warm milk, the only kind safe for children to drink, Mrs. Jefferson insisted. Outside the kitchen was a "stew," a small fishpond where the fish caught in the river one day could swim about until time to be cooked the next day.

Jenny Jefferson set a table-board in the dining room with a "board cloth" to cover it. Most pioneering families had no china plates but ate from pewter dishes and bowls. The Jeffersons drank "dishes" of tea and chocolate from cups that had no handles. They probably had some silver spoons and forks and perhaps other pieces of silver, since neither Peter nor Jane Randolph had come from poor families. Jenny never put flowers in the center of the table-board. Instead, she made "a grand conceit," piling high, in a special dish, foods that could be eaten, like tiny cakes, fruits, nutmeats, or candied flowers.

Mr. and Mrs. Jefferson knew that many farmers around them had none of the luxuries they had. Farm families ate from wooden trenchers instead of plates. Trenchers were square pieces of wood with shallow hollows scraped out to hold the food. When a mother said, "Now eat a square meal," she was talking about eating from a trencher. The children did not get any dessert until they had finished what was on the trencher, because they had to turn it upside down to make a clean plate for the next part of the meal.

Some of the neighbors had only a few chairs, and their children had to stand up to eat their food. Poor families rarely had sugar, tea, or coffee and never drank hot chocolate. Instead of the pigeon pies, roast partridge, and turkey that the Jefferson children had for dinner, poor children were lucky to have rabbit, bread and milk, and, in the spring, the leaves of the poke plant for greens. Only young poke leaves were safe. The plant was poisonous late in summer.

The Jeffersons had plenty of well-to-do neighbors near Shadwell. Within ten miles of the Rivanna Water Gap were several plantations owned by Virginians who were related to them distantly or by marriage. Every time a horseman approached the house, Mrs. Jefferson warned her cook that there might be company for dinner. John Harvie came to visit from Belmont. Nicholas Meriwether came from The Farm until he died, when he willed the land to his grandson Nicholas Lewis. Joshua Fry, who traveled often with Peter Jefferson, lived at Viewmont on a nearby river. The Walkers might drop in from their plantation at Castle Hill or Edward Carter from Blenheim. But Jenny Jefferson rarely saw their wives or any other lady.

Living far out in the country, the Jeffersons as well as their neighbors could expect that almost anyone who dropped in would stay for a meal and probably spend the night. Often there were not enough beds, but men crowded two or three into one bed without complaining. The children had great fun sleeping on the floor in the hallway. No Virginian would have thought of not inviting a visitor to stay as long as he liked. But Southern hospitality was not limited to friends. Some who stopped were total strangers, just passing through. They knew that even if they could find one of the few taverns by the road, they would have to share their bed with bedbugs and one or two other men. Staying in a nice home was much more comfortable.

"Besides," one traveler wrote his friends at home, "in Virginia a man needs no money at all except to pay for the ferries."

The hosts did, however, have ways of cutting short what looked like too long a visit. At one home a guest had goose for dinner the first night, and for every meal including breakfast the second and third days. The fourth night, dinner was "goose hash." The guest took the hint and departed. Another visitor says, "Every day at dinner we had a good bottle of wine first, and then a bottle of bad." One older man complained that he and a friend were bedded in a room next door to the nursery and could not sleep for the baby crying all night. He left early the next day.

In November 1744, young Tom Jefferson had to leave the cradle to make room for a baby sister, Elizabeth. No one knows how soon the family discovered that the pretty little baby was mentally handicapped. But Elizabeth was loved and protected by all the Jefferson children. A severe earthquake struck one day when Elizabeth was

a young lady. She was so frightened that she ran into the woods and the Jeffersons could not find her for three days. She lived only a few days longer.

As of the first of January 1745, Shadwell was in a new county called Albemarle. Peter Jefferson, Joshua Fry, William Randolph, and others who owned land there went to the first county meeting. Fry was appointed county surveyor. Randolph was made the clerk. Jefferson became lieutenant colonel of the county militia. They talked of building a new town near Shadwell to be the county seat.

"See," Jefferson reported happily to his wife, "we don't live in the wilderness any more. Perhaps even the Randolphs will move up here some day."

Then one day that summer a tired rider on a sweaty horse galloped up to Shadwell's door to ask for Master Jefferson.

"Master Randolph is dying, sir," gasped the rider. "Can you come at once?"

Peter Jefferson ordered his servant to pack some clothing and follow. He leaped onto his horse and took off for Tuckahoe without even changing his shirt. He had to reach Randolph in time to renew his promise.

3

Wilderness Journey

"BUT why do we have to move?" five-year-old Jane Jefferson kept asking. "Why can't Judith and Mary and Thomas Mann Randolph come to live at our house?"

Only two-year-old Tom and tiny Elizabeth seemed not to care that the Jeffersons were moving. The past two days their father had spent deciding which of the slaves should go with them to Tuckahoe and which should stay at Shadwell to run the plantation. Now he tried once more to help his small daughters understand the move that was to take his family away from their mountains for the next few years.

"I promised Mr. Randolph that we would live all together as one family in their home. It's a large house, much grander than ours. We'll be together there just as we are here at Shadwell."

He looked to his wife for help.

"This is going to be one of those adventures you have always wanted to go on," Jenny told the children. She did not have to pretend her excitement. Moving to Tuckahoe meant for her a trip back to the gentle life she had known before her marriage. "Tomorrow we will all become explorers and ride through the wilderness, just the way your father does when he and Mr. Fry go out to survey land. And for two nights you children will sleep under the stars."

The girls shouted their approval. They lay back on the floor before the fire to sleep, with a drowsy-eyed Tom between them. The slaves had already tied their comfortable feather bedding onto one of the wagons and packed the many household articles that Mrs. Jefferson refused to leave behind her.

Odd, Peter Jefferson thought, he never would really understand women. He knew that his wife was far more suited to the tea parties and dances of the Tidewater country than to the rough manners and poor farmers she met here in the mountains. Yet even she had watched longingly this night as the last rays of the sun faded behind the Blue Ridge Mountains.

"Time to go," Jenny called the children from breakfast when daylight quieted the noisy night ravens. For a moment, giving Shadwell a last look, she felt the same sort of pangs as when she had sailed from England in her father's ship.

The next moment, Mr. Jefferson swung into his saddle and gave final orders to John Dawson, his overseer, for the slaves who were to stay behind. Jane and Mary perched in a nest of hay in one wagon. They each wore large sunbonnets and gloves to keep their hands white. Around their necks hung the face masks their mother had warned them to pull up over their noses as soon as the sun came up. No Virginia lady allowed the sun to tan her face or hands as if she worked in the fields. Father and mother planned to take turns carrying baby Elizabeth. Young Tom rode on horseback, held securely on a soft pillow by a slave. It had been his father's decision that Tom should ride like a man rather than sit with the girls and their slave nurses. For that reason Thomas Jefferson remembered his ride on that horse all the rest of his life.

The slaves staying at Shadwell stood on the top of the hill, waving until the small wagon and horse train was out of sight. Their feelings were mixed. For some this meant a breaking up of their own loved families. Some, like Sally the cook, choked back tears as they kissed loved ones good-bye. She was pleased that the Jeffersons wanted her to go with them to Tuckahoe, but it was hard to leave her older children, who had to stay behind. She felt lucky that Mr. Jefferson had allowed her younger children to go with her.

The wagons jolted over rocks and logs. They followed the Three-Notched Road for only a short way, then branched off on what looked to Jenny like no more than an Indian trail.

"That's exactly what it is," said her husband. "There is no wagon road yet that goes to Tuckahoe. We'll have to make it as we go."

The slaves whacked at bushes where the trail was too narrow for the wagons. When they came to wading-deep streams, the oxen pulled their loads through the water. But when they came to swimming-deep streams, they had to follow along the water's edge until the wagons came to a place shallow enough to cross safely. Rocky roads turned to red mud, and mud soon gave way to thick underbrush.

Sometimes Mrs. Jefferson left her horse to ride in the hay with the girls. Then Jane rode her mother's horse beside Tom. She talked to him and made him laugh at her funny faces. Jane had a way with smaller children that made Tom follow her every move. When he was tired, his sister's songs always made him happy.

"We'll noon in this spot," Mr. Jefferson announced at last to a tired family. The place he chose had good grass and water for the horses and a dry field where the children could run and stretch their legs. Sally, the cook, immediately set about ordering the other slaves to lay the board with food she had prepared before leaving Shadwell.

"She's a better overseer than the one we have," Mrs. Jefferson whispered to her husband. "I never saw any of them move faster."

Before long they were all eating a dinner as good as those Sally cooked at home. The Jeffersons had time for a rest while the slaves repacked the wagons.

Traveling through wild country was nothing new to Jefferson, but having dinner beside a stream with a board cloth on a table and pewter plates was new. He told the family about the trips he and William Randolph had made into the Blue Ridge Mountains to see the land they had bought together along the Sherrando River. He recalled surveying trips when he had carried so many instruments there was little space for food. On those trips a man was lucky to have along some salted beef and a dry cube of portable soup he could mix with river water for his dinner. Jefferson usually made the trip to Tuckahoe in a day. With the family and the wagons, he figured they moved about four miles in an hour. They would probably make Tuckahoe in two nights and three days, unless the wagons broke down.

Making a comfortable bed in the wagon with his wife beside him that night was new too. Surveyors usually found soft pine

branches to lie on, stretching out their feet toward the fire on a cold night to keep from freezing.

"One night," he told Jenny, "we had a young helper who was lazy. While we cut fresh pine branches to sleep on, this boy, Jeremiah, used some branches already cut. During the night a spark flew onto his dry branches and set his bed on fire. We woke him up, of course, so he wouldn't get burned, but we managed to let him get scared enough."

In the morning the slaves had no trouble finding the horses because each one had a bell tied to its halter in case it wandered in the dark. Horses could not be tied all night because they sickened if they could not move through the grass and nibble. The gentle sound of the horses' bells as they moved had lulled the family to

sleep. The next day's travel was less rocky. One of the slaves brought treasures for the children to see.

"Virginny catchfly, Miss Jane and Miss Mary," said Old Ben, showing them the sticky stem that trapped flies and held them fast. Another time Old Ben found them some mushrooms, which he said were called "Indian bread." Old Ben had been on many wilderness trips with Mr. Jefferson and was proud of his knowledge.

Just before they went to bed that night they heard a terrifying noise.

"That sounded like our old bull bellowing," said Jane.

"What was it?" the children wondered. They were glad this was their last night for sleeping outside. But their father just laughed.

"That's Virginia bells."

"Bells?" they all echoed.

"That's what we call Virginia frogs. They're just saying good night."

The third day, while they were nooning, Mrs. Jefferson thought she must be seeing things. It couldn't be, but it looked like a coach pulled by two sleek horses! Not many Virginians owned a coach, but somehow the slaves from Tuckahoe had managed the loan of one and had driven out to welcome them.

The children clambered into the coach and snuggled into the soft seats. Their mother ran her hand gently along the smooth leather to be sure she wasn't dreaming. A long time had passed since she had felt such a luxury.

"I'm going to like Tuckahoe," said Mary quietly.

The rest of the trip seemed to go very fast. The tired travelers dozed, waking only when the horses came to a stop. Mrs. Jefferson hurried to straighten her bonnet and adjust her traveling dress.

"Wait, Jane," she instructed as the coach door was opened from outside. "You might as well begin learning this minute. Our mountain manners will not do here in the Tidewater. After I get out, you get out. But not as if you were tumbling out of a tree. Watch and do as I do. And Mary, you follow Jane. Tom, you get out last."

Jenny stepped out with baby Elizabeth. The girls followed their mother primly and one of the Randolph slaves, wearing a bright blue and gold uniform, lifted Tom out and set him firmly on the ground. The brick and frame Randolph mansion was the largest building any of the children had ever seen.

4

Seven Cousins Meet

STANDING at the bottom of the steps, waiting to greet them, were the orphans the Jeffersons had come to live with. Judith, who was nine, had a firm grasp on the hand of her seven-year-old sister, Mary. Thomas Mann, who at four was the owner of the mansion and all the slaves on the plantation, stood by himself.

"Welcome home," said the Randolph children politely. They bowed and curtseyed to their elders and shook hands solemnly with the children. But as soon as they all went inside they became children again, clattering up the stairs to show their cousins the secrets of the big house they were to share. Peter and Jenny Jefferson were shown into the withdrawing room, where some of the Randolph uncles were waiting to talk to them.

Tuckahoe stood on a low hill overlooking the James River near where Tuckahoe Creek entered the river. No house could have been better designed for two families to live in. It had two large wings joined by a long saloon, forming the shape of the letter H. Each wing was two stories high with four rooms on each floor. The saloon had a very high ceiling and a chandelier with a hundred candles. In summer, with all the long windows open and a breeze blowing through, the saloon seemed the coolest spot in Virginia.

The children's tour included every hidden staircase and even a secret room in the mansion. Then they explored the outbuildings.

One was a carpenter's shop; one had the blacksmith's forge. Another was the kitchen, where Sally was already starting to make hoecake for the slaves' dinner. The fourth building was just being painted.

"It's going to be our school," Judith Randolph explained.

Soon after the family moved into Tuckahoe, the Jeffersons gave a large dinner party. All the plantation owners around were invited to meet the new residents, even though many already knew Peter and Jenny Jefferson. Inviting the neighbors to share the pleasure of a new home, or even an old one redecorated, was an old Virginia custom. From that time on, the family went to parties all year. In summer there were fish feasts and barbecues, held picnic style on the lawns that overlooked the James River. When Peter Jefferson was young, each family had brought food to the party, but now that the planters had so much slave help, bringing food to a party was no longer the custom. In winter the neighbors had teas and balls for the newcomers at Tuckahoe.

The family soon grew beyond the original seven children. The year after they moved to Tuckahoe, Tom's little sister Martha was born. In all his life Tom Jefferson never got over being part of a large family. When he was older, he invited this sister—with her six children to move into his home. Later he asked his daughter with her large family to live with him at Monticello. He was happiest living in a crowd.

Young Tom loved being surrounded by playmates. They played Hide the Thimble and Grind the Bottle. The older girls played Checks with peach stones. Thomas Mann had a popgun made from a branch of the elder tree that Tom Jefferson played with when his cousin wasn't looking. Later, Old Ben made Tom a popgun of his own. On rainy days, they tried Blindman's Bluff or played with Thomas Mann's clay marbles.

Children on Southern plantations were free to run and play without many rules. Unlike the children in New England states, who were punished for playing too much or for making noise on Sunday, Virginia children had a carefree childhood. They played often with the slave children until they grew older. One by one, as they grew up, their black friends had to go to work instead of playing or going to school. Gradually the plantation children learned why their black friends always called them Master Tom and Miss Jane.

A few miles from Tuckahoe was Manakin town, once a village of the Monacan Indians. Now it was filled with French people called "refugees," a new word in America.

"Refugee means 'sheltered people,' " Peter told Tom one day. "Our king gave this piece of land to these people because they had to run away from their own country."

Tom's father had always told him a man should never run away from his own problems but should stay and face them.

"They would die if they had stayed. You see, they wanted to worship God in one way and their king told them they would have to worship God only in his way. In the colonies they have the freedom to worship any way they please—as long as they pay their taxes to the English church."

Peter Jefferson was sorry he had added that last bit about the taxes. Tom worried all day about the people of Manakin Town who were given the freedom to worship with one hand while another hand reached out and took money back from them.

"They should not have to pay for our church," Tom said, after thinking it over for a while.

About eight miles from Tuckahoe, a new town, to be called Richmond, was just being built. Lots and streets had been laid out, but only a few people had built homes there. Most planters preferred living away from towns. Not even the capitol, Williamsburg, had many families who lived there all year. Richmond was on the James River, but since it was above the falls line, large ships could not reach it. Merchants were slow to build shops in a town where ships could not dock.

Shortly after Tom Jefferson turned five, the subject of school came up. Mr. Jefferson had hired a tutor to see that the girls, as well as the boys, learned to read, write, and cypher, which meant learning to reckon in numbers. For three years Tom had toddled after the older children, wishing he could go to school with them. Often he had sat on the step listening as they recited their lessons aloud. He already knew the alphabet of 24 letters by heart, as well as the different forms for two of them. (The letter *I* had two forms, a short *I* and a long *I*, now called a *J*. And the letter *U* was sometimes pointed, a form now called *V*.)

The schoolmaster slept in a tiny room in the schoolhouse, but he took meals with the family. Only the older children were allowed to eat at the family table. Until children had perfect table manners,

they ate in a small room by themselves. After dinner all the children were allowed to meet the family guests. One spring day Joshua Fry was paying a call. All the children liked Mr. Fry. Besides being a surveyor, he taught mathematics at William and Mary College in Williamsburg. He had a way of talking to children that made them feel grown up. As usual, this afternoon he had a problem he hoped they would help him solve.

"Which of you boys can help me?" he said to Tom Jefferson and Thomas Mann. "I am taking home seven beautiful apples, but I have only two children to give them to. How can I give them the apples without making one mad because I gave the other one more?"

"You could eat one yourself," suggested Thomas Mann.

"Cut one in half?" asked Tom Jefferson.

"Two excellent ideas," said Fry.

"Master Tom has a good mind, Mr. Jefferson," said the school-master later.

"He does," said Jenny Jefferson, "but isn't it dangerous for a young brain to be overworked too early in life?"

"He's right, Jenny," her husband interrupted. "Tom is ready for school." Jenny knew better than to say another word. Decisions about the children were entirely up to the father. She knew she should just be happy that Peter was not planning to send Tom to England for his education.

Tom was not at all sure, now that the chance had come, that he really wanted to go to school. He did want to be with the older children. But part of him knew there would be no more time to ride on the horse in front of his father on trips around the plantation

or to play pirates and have hurtleberry-throwing wars with his friend Jupiter.

"I will be away from home many weeks this summer anyway, Tom," his father told him. "Mr. Fry and I will be surveying some boundary lines so we can make a map of Virginia."

"Can Jupiter go to school with me?" Tom asked. There was a moment of silence before Peter recalled that Jupiter was the slave boy Tom played with so often. Tom hurried to add, "He's just as old as I am, and he's right smart."

His father explained gently that slave children never went to school. Tom burst into tears of frustration. He remembered the scene long after he grew up. But that day he said only that when he was a man, he would see that all slave children went to school. And then they would be set free and sent out with tools to start their own farms.

The next morning Jane Jefferson grasped the hand of a tearful small brother and led him up the steps into the schoolhouse. Only Elizabeth and baby Martha were left behind.

5

Pupils or Apprentices

WILLIAM Randolph had left instructions for his son's school and asked that his daughters be "educated according to their quality and circumstances." But poor children had no way to go to school without money.

Before the Revolution, Virginia had no middle class. People were either low class (vulgar) or high class (educated and rich). Most parents wanted their children to learn to read and write and cypher. But because the plantations were so large, the people could not start a local school system. The schoolhouse would be several hours' ride from the children's homes.

When a poor family grew so large that parents did not have enough food to feed all the children, the father or mother took their oldest child to be apprenticed. A child could be apprenticed at any age—even a few months old—but usually he or she was about six.

"It's the best thing we can do for the boy," a father would insist when the mother cried. "He'll learn a trade, his master will teach him to read and write and cypher, and we'll have someone to make us proud in our old age."

The apprentice went to live with the master's family, but since this was not their own child, they never wasted time coddling a mere apprentice. The master gave a boy the mean jobs to do while teaching him carpentry or barrelmaking or tending horses. A girl apprentice learned "the art of housewifery," which meant she did all the menial work around the master's house.

A boy apprentice lived with his master until he was twenty-one years old. A girl left when she was eighteen, unless she married before then. Usually apprentices lived in a different town from their parents and were lucky if they saw their own family once a year. Apprenticeship was a hard school.

Benjamin Franklin published a book in 1749 written just for apprentice boys and called *A Present For An Apprentice*. Franklin had once been an apprentice himself. He knew there were plenty of books for rich, educated boys, but none had ever been published for a "young man of low station" to help him learn how to succeed and perhaps become rich some day.

"First, never lie," the book warns. "You'll always be found out in the end." People in those days felt they could spot a criminal by his ugly face. The apprentice was also warned to be careful to guard the secrets of the family he lived in and to keep his own secrets. He had to be careful of his master's money and his own. And he should choose for friends only those young people that he could learn something from.

Virginia colony had almost no "free" schools, except for one grammar school for boys in Williamsburg. Farmers near a small town sometimes went together and hired a tutor and set up a school building in an old field—one that had been worn out from growing tobacco. But the children who attended the "old field" school had to pay the tutor a few pence every month. In the backcountry most farmers rarely had even ten pence in their hands all year. When they wanted to buy sugar, they traded corn for it, or traded a beaver skin for a pair of boots.

Jacob Moon, an overseer, hired a young man named Devereux Jarrett to live at his house and teach the Moon children. Jarrett was a simple person, with the humble attitude many English had toward their betters.

"I looked on gentlefolk as beings of a superior order," said Jarrett. "I was quite shy of them and kept off at a humble distance."

But at the end of a year's teaching, Jarrett had been paid only seven pounds, hardly enough to buy himself a warm coat. The next year he took a job on a plantation teaching the children of one of the "gentlefolk." They paid him fifteen pounds a year.

Rich boys and girls had more choice in schools. Those who lived on a plantation could have a tutor live in and teach them, as the Randolph and Jefferson children had at Tuckahoe. Or they could go to a boarding school or a private school in town. Boys usually went to one school, while their sisters went to a "Dame school" in some gentlewoman's home, where they were sure to learn more art, music, and needlework than geography. Parsons often ran boarding schools to help support their families. The final choice was to be sent to England.

At a parson's school, students lived with the preacher's family, sharing their food and fasts. Parsons were noted for being stingy when it came to the comforts of life. A shortage of food in the kitchen might result in the parson's declaring a fast "to prevent the pestilence of Europe from coming to the colonies" or for any other worthy reason. The parson taught his students reading, writing, arithmetic, geography, and history. Some even taught Latin and Greek. A heavy dose of religion and church attendance was thrown in for good measure.

At least one of Tom's friends was sent to a classical boarding school to learn Latin and Greek. The boy's parents were afraid their son might not find a suitable wife (one with money) or position in life if he had not learned to read the classics. And he had to know Latin and Greek to go to college, because most college courses were taught in those languages. When Tom's friend wrote home letters in proper Latin, his mother cried because she could not read them. Girls never learned those languages because they could never go to college.

The best education, many Virginians felt, was available only in England. Yet wealthy planters in the 1750s were no longer agreed. Many said an English education was not worth the price—and the price was very high.

Children left home very young, some less than a year old, in the care of a ship's captain. The trip to England might last two months and was certainly dangerous. In England the captain deposited the children with relatives who were to send them off to a proper boarding school. By the time the children returned home to America, ten or fifteen years later, they were complete strangers to their family and their country.

Not all children were lucky enough to return. And many came home from cold, damp English boarding schools with consumption, a disease for which there was no cure. Often children died in England of smallpox. That disease seemed especially deadly for children from the colonies.

There was another reason, rarely discussed in the colonies, for not sending the children to England. The English children teased them without mercy, because their parents looked down on the "colonials." Criminals who were given the choice between going to the New World or being hanged in England often chose hanging. When a wealthy Virginia planter, William Byrd, proposed marriage to a lady in England, her father asked how much money he had.

"I own one hundred and sixty thousand acres of land in Virginia," he answered.

The father refused to allow his daughter to marry Byrd. When Byrd asked the lady why, she answered, "My father says owning land off this Island [England] is about as worthless as having land on the moon."

Many parents felt as William Randolph and Peter Jefferson did. They wanted their sons to learn everything possible about the new world they lived in. They didn't need to know dead languages to run plantations. They needed to know mathematics, so they could keep business accounts straight. They needed to know surveying. And every man should know the law.

"Laws seem to be made for the rich man. A poor man rarely gets a fair break," Jefferson told his son once. "Laws are like spiders' webs, which entangle the small flies—while the great ones break through them."

6

Copybooks & Dancing Class

"WAKE up, Tom," insisted a loud voice. "You'll be late to school."

School? But there was not going to be any more school. Six-year-old Tom Jefferson had taken care of that matter the day before. He had run away from the schoolmaster at Tuckahoe to a private place behind one of the outbuildings. There he had carefully recited the Lord's Prayer and arranged with God to close down school forever.

For close to a year now he had submitted meekly to the tyranny of the schoolmaster. Since Peter Jefferson was often gone on long surveying trips, the schoolmaster had the last word on what Tom was allowed and not allowed to do. His father would have understood the need for a fishing expedition up Tuckahoe Creek or the importance of building a raft to float across the James River with Thomas Mann. But the schoolmaster's trips to the great outdoors were limited to the three times a day he sprinted over to the main house for his meals.

Tom couldn't go to his mother with his upsets. Jenny Jefferson had been in tears all winter. A little brother, Peter, had been born in October, but he had lived only about five weeks, and his funeral was very sad.

Then one day a visiting parson came for Sunday dinner. He told the children that if they said their prayers, God would answer them. This morning Tom lay abed, perfectly confident that the parson had shown him the way to get out of school.

"Tom's just pretending he can't hear," said his cousin Thomas Mann Randolph. "Just like he did yesterday when the schoolmaster told him to recite and Tom couldn't say one word."

"Hush, Thomas Mann," said Jane. "Do get up, little brother."

From the cozy depths of the feather bed he shared with his cousin Thomas Mann, Tom Jefferson was aware of the waking up noises made by his sisters and Randolph cousins, all in different stages of scrubbing and dressing for school.

"There won't be any school," he advised them sleepily.

The girls laughed, and Jane began singing a song about no more school. Judy and Mary Randolph helped the Jefferson girls to pull Tom from his warm spot and send him off to the washbowl.

All the way to the schoolhouse, Tom followed the older children, certain that when they arrived, they would discover he was right. But as they approached the door, the master walked out stiffly with a "Good morning" for each one of them.

Tom stared for a moment before he snatched off his cap and bowed.

"Good morning, sir."

Thomas Mann made an "I told you so" face as they sat down. Parents didn't answer prayers, Tom had discovered when he had begged his father not to send him to school any more. But God? That was supposed to be His job, wasn't it? What was Tom to do the next time his throat closed down on his words? He had no trouble talking to his family, but when it came to speaking about something that was really important, or reciting at school, Tom could never make the words come out the way he wanted them to sound.

Perhaps if they ever moved back to Shadwell, things would be easier. He had heard Jane and even his mother say life was easier there. Thomas remembered nothing about his mountain home. In fact, he was not even sure what mountains looked like, since the Tidewater country around Tuckahoe had only low hills.

"Frontier country" Thomas Mann had called Shadwell. "There's wild Indians and tiger cats, and people live in ugly log houses."

"That's not true!" Tom shouted. "Besides, tiger cats don't live in this country. My father says they're called mountain lions."

"Your father lets wild Indians pitch their tents on his land. Old Ben told me so."

"They are his friends," Tom shouted back. "And Shadwell is not ugly logs. It's . . . beautiful." He felt his throat tighten with emotion. He had not the least idea whether Shadwell was really beautiful, but then neither did his cousin.

"Not like my house," argued Thomas Mann. When Thomas Mann said "My House" in just that way, Tom always got too angry for words. Now that Thomas Mann had turned eight, he never let any of the children forget they were living in his house.

The school at Tuckahoe was called an English school, because the children learned reading, writing, and arithmetic. Their schoolmaster didn't know Latin or Greek, so the boys would have to get a classical education later from another tutor.

The school bell rang at seven, so there was an hour of lessons before breakfast. The schoolmaster said the children's brains were at their highest peak early in the morning, before they became dulled by food. For that reason he taught the hardest lessons first. The girls read from the Bible and wrote essays. For Thomas Mann and Tom, the hardest lesson was mathematics. Because speaking in front of others was torture for Tom Jefferson, the master always made him recite aloud.

"Four farthings make one pence . . . twelve pence make one shilling . . . twenty sh—"

"Speak up, Master Tom. We can't hear you."

"—shillings make a p-pound."

The bell to go to the main house never rang soon enough to spare Tom from embarrassment that flushed his face beet red.

After breakfast, the children returned to the schoolroom until the dinner bell rang at noon, giving them plenty of time to clean up before the big meal of the day. School began again about three and ended at five.

The boys wrote on slates, but the girls were starting to use paper and quill pens. Because of the grunts and groans coming from their side of the room, Tom was in no hurry to try that exercise.

Each girl rubbed her paper with a piece of cotton dipped in a fine powder called pounce, so the paper would hold the ink. Then she dipped her quill in the homemade ink and made the same letter over and over until a page was filled.

"No, no, Miss Jane. The upward strokes as fine as a hair, only the downward strokes may be full. . . . Don't lift your pen . . . elbow close to body . . . rest your hand on the end of your little finger . . ."

The girls struggled, never pleasing their tutor. They spent most of their writing time scratching out their inky mistakes with a penknife and then rubbing pounce on the paper again so they could write over their mistakes. The fine powder covered their aprons like road dust.

Some days the routine changed, especially now that the girls were getting older. Judith, Jane, and the two Marys were excused from book learning to take lessons in needlework. The teacher was a widow lady who traveled from one plantation to the next showing young ladies how to handle a needle and turn out fancy stitches. When Tom heard his sisters complaining about the boredom of making pen wipers and hemming pocket handkerchiefs, he was glad to be a boy, even though it meant reading harder books than his sisters read.

A few times a year a drawing master came to teach the girls art. He stayed about a week and then, having made artists of them all, moved on to another planter's family.

The music master, who came six times a year, was the most popular of all. The girls each had lessons playing the Randolph harpsichord. Jane Jefferson loved singing especially, and Tom used to stand outside the room just to hear her sweet voice.

"Ut . . . re . . . mi . . . fa . . . sol . . . la." The scales Jane sang had only those notes.

One day the music master invited Tom inside the saloon and showed him a violin. When the master drew the bow over the strings, something inside Tom felt instantly at peace. But when he drew the bow across the strings, that magic something was missing.

"It will come with practice, Master Tom," said the music master, kindly hiding the effect Tom's music had on him. "Keep trying."

Tom did keep trying. The violin brought him a kind of pleasure he had never felt before. Long after the music master had left to take music to the children on some other plantation, Tom was still trying to make sounds like those he had first heard come from the instrument. The family sent him to the top floor of the other wing to practice until he succeeded. At the end of a frustrating school day, when he had to recite aloud in school and the words had not come out right, Tom picked up his violin and let it speak for him.

"You are spending too much time on your music, Master Tom," his schoolmaster barked one day.

The schoolmaster put the girls to work sewing together pieces of paper to make copybooks for both boys and girls to use. They wrote in them endless phrases to memorize, struggling against splattering their homemade ink across the page or thickening an upward stroke instead of the downward stroke with their quill pens:

Confidence in an unfaithful friend is like a broken tooth. . . . In the morning think what you have to do, and at night ask yourself what you have done. . . . Love your neighbor as yourself and your country more than self.

One of Tom's favorite subjects was philosophy, or what schools today call science. But Tom's 1750 science lessons were not very accurate.

"Reptiles are animals or insects that rest on one part of their body while advancing forward with the rest, like earthworms, snakes, and caterpillars," he recited after his tutor. "Rattlesnakes in America make such a loud noise when they move that people can run away when they hear the snakes coming."

"Is that true, Father?" he asked Peter Jefferson one day. "Can you really hear a rattlesnake coming?"

His father, who had come across many rattlesnakes on his trips through the mountains, almost dropped the book he was reading.

"Where on earth did you learn that falsehood?"

The tutor, who was sitting nearby, said it was printed right in a philosophy book he had found in the Randolph library.

Few men valued books as much as Peter Jefferson. He had forty books of his own at Shadwell. But he knew what to do with this one.

"Bring me the book immediately," he demanded. "If it has any more such tripe in it, it will be thrown away. Meanwhile, I suggest you read to the children from a book that we know is accurate."

After that Tom checked many facts with his father when the family gathered together in the evening.

"Is it true that plants and flowers here can never grow so large or lovely as those in England, Father? The schoolmaster says they can't because they have grown in a savage state since the beginning of time and cannot ever catch up."

"Oh, no," his mother gasped before his father could answer. "Virginia is famous for its kitchen gardens. We grow vegetables and flowers almost the year round here. I can remember only three or four months in England when we could eat fresh vegetables."

"Well, what about the wild beasts? The tutor said that American bears and wolves and elks are not able to defend themselves because their teeth and horns are not strong."

Peter Jefferson came near to taking that young tutor with him on his next trip into the mountains to let him test the strength of an American wolf's teeth. And Tom spent many years as an adult still arguing: American wildlife was *not* more puny than that found in Europe. It was untrue that America's climate, which can go from cool to very hot in just one day, was unhealthy, or that children who grew up in America would be shorter than English children and turn the color of the Indians.

Tom wished that someone would write a book about North America and the animals, birds, flowers, and trees that lived in the New World. So far everything he had read about America had been written by men who just visited for a few months and then went back to England to write about it.

Virginia had no public libraries. Schoolmasters had to rely on the few books they had bought when they were in school or to hope that a plantation owner would let them read books from his own private library. Most books had to be shipped from England, and months went by between the ordering of a book and its arrival by ship. Meanwhile Tom and the other students had to make their own books by writing down rules for spelling and mathematics in their copybooks.

When Tom Jefferson and Thomas Mann Randolph finally learned to "cypher to the rule of three," they had gone as far as their tutor could teach. For most students, this rule was like a diploma—once they had learned it and the arithmetic that led up to it, they were considered educated.

The rule of three meant being able to find a fourth number from three given numbers. For example: if three men spend 20 pounds in 10 days, how much will they spend in 25 days? Or if three yards of cloth cost 8 shillings, what is the price of 15 yards?

Here is how Tom's answer looked:

40 shillings at £2

Yds	Shillings	Yds
3	8	15
	15	
3	120	40

Tom Jefferson was eight before he saw his first real dance. Judith and Mary Randolph had become young ladies almost overnight. For the past few years a dancing master had come to Tuckahoe several times a year. He gave individual lessons to each of the young people, including the boys. Tom and Thomas Mann faced dancing class with all the enthusiasm of a criminal facing the whipping post. But when they complained to Peter Jefferson, he persuaded them it was a necessary part of their education and should be borne as bravely as being bled when they were sick.

As soon as the pupils had learned some basic steps and knew how ladies and gentlemen must behave in a ballroom, the dancing master made out a schedule for dancing classes to take place at different plantations. The Randolph girls behaved as if they had just been waiting for this magic time of their lives. Jane and Mary Jefferson counted the hours until they were old enough to attend. The boys were overjoyed to learn that they were still too young to be invited to this formal dance lesson. They didn't even feel guilty that their sisters would have no boys to dance with.

The first afternoon that the dancing class was held at Tuckahoe, the boys watched from a distance. Their sisters seemed to have gone out of their minds. They had spent days planning how to crape their hair, trying on their party dresses, begging to be allowed to wear jewelry. Even Mrs. Jefferson was flushed pink with excitement. An hour before the class was to begin, carriages came up the drive and attendants unloaded mothers and young people from the other plantations where the dancing master taught.

"There are boys, too!" Tom whispered to his cousin from their hiding place in the bushes. Neither boy had thought his sisters might allow strangers to be their dancing partners.

They watched as the boys stood in one awkward group, taking out their watches and trying to remember to keep their hands out of their pockets. The girls stood in another group, giggling and pretending deep conversation. Finally the dancing master appeared and ushered them into the saloon to begin class. For over an hour he taught each pupil individually a new step while the others watched. One giggle or whisper from the watchers earned them a hard smack on the shoulder. After time out for dinner, the dance began in earnest. All afternoon Tom listened happily to the violin and harpsichord accompanying the minuet, reels, and country dances.

The parents sat on the "sophas" and chairs enjoying the event and thinking a few years ahead as they watched the sons and daughters of some of the first families of Virginia. Children did not fall in love and marry whomever they pleased. They were carefully thrown together with "the right sort" and never allowed to meet "the wrong sort." Dancing class was an important first step. By six, the class ended, the dancers put on their traveling clothes, and the coaches pulled up to the door to take them all home again.

Life at Tuckahoe was coming to a close, now that the Randolph girls were growing up. Peter and Jenny Jefferson did not need the dancing class to show them that Judith and Mary Randolph would be thinking of marriage in a few years. The Randolph uncles now invited the girls to visit at their plantations often so they could meet the right young men. This was especially important to the Randolphs, because their own sister had fallen in love and married an overseer without their father's permission. Even though the unacceptable husband had died a few years later and the widow then married a young man of the right sort, the experience had been a disaster for the Randolph family.

No girl married without her father or guardian's permission. A young man asked a girl's permission to "wait on her," and if she agreed, he could hope she might like him. Then a gentleman went to her father to begin the financial arrangements. Father asked how much land the young man had and how much money he had. The father then told him how much land or money he intended to settle on his daughter, but only if the young man were acceptable to him. Judith and Mary would have to obtain their uncles' permission to marry.

Their own problems, too, prompted the Jeffersons to think about leaving. In October 1751 one of the slaves, Robin, had run away from Shadwell. A young troublemaker with crooked legs, Robin had been wearing an iron collar when he had grabbed a gun and run. Peter Jefferson feared he had been away too long from overseeing his own land and slaves.

Mrs. Jefferson was expecting another baby in October 1752. The Jeffersons had already buried two infant sons in Tidewater country. Jenny was ready for the peace and quiet of their mountain home.

All the Jeffersons packed for the trip back to Shadwell. Everyone, that is, except Tom. He was not going home just yet.

7

Tom at Boarding School

GOOD-BYES were hard to say. Peter Jefferson had finally persuaded nine-year-old Tom that going to a boarding school was an important part of his growing up.

"Too many women around you," said his father. "You'll grow soft if you go back to Shadwell with us now. And besides, there are no schools in our county where you can find the sort of learning you need."

Tom promised to write letters home every chance he had. But no coaches went toward Shadwell, and the only way to send his family a letter was by someone he knew was riding up that way.

"You write something down every day," Peter Jefferson instructed his son. "Tell us what books you read, who your friends are, everything. Then when someone stops by to pick up a letter from you, it will be already written and that person will not have to delay his trip while you agonize over an empty sheet of paper about what to write.

"Yes sir," Tom agreed. Then, after a hug for each member of his family, he vaulted up on his horse. His father rode with him the five miles from Tuckahoe to Dover Church.

"Don't disappoint us, son. We have great hopes for you," he said when they arrived at Reverend Douglass's parsonage. The house that had looked large before, when the children attended the church nearby, now looked tiny when Tom realized how many students were to live in it with the parson's large family. Surrounding the house were outbuildings for the kitchen, barn, stable, dairy, meat house, and corn house. Drab mud walls enclosed the kitchen garden.

"Anger and laziness are the vices you will have to watch out for," Peter Jefferson was saying. "Anger will only serve to torment you. And laziness brings on boredom, which will make your body sick. Don't forget to keep your body exercised as well as your mind."

Tom only half heard his father's words, and yet they struck some furrow of his brain, because he was to give the same advice to his own children when they went away to school many years later.

Tom Jefferson spent almost nine months a year at Dover Church for the next five years. Board and tuition cost 16 pounds sterling. Yet he remembered very little about the school to tell his children afterward, except that he had learned Latin and Greek and advanced mathematics. He learned French, perhaps from one of the refugees who lived in Manakin town, since the French language would have sounded very strange through the Scottish accent of the Reverend Douglass.

The students read the *Virginia Gazette* to learn what was going on in the world. But since the colony had only one newspaper, they learned only one side of the news, the side the government wanted them to hear. Most of the paper's four pages were about events going on in Europe. Tom Jefferson wished that news of events happening in Virginia and the other colonies filled more space. That way the colonists would feel closer to each other.

The newspaper did not even mention that the day after September 2, 1752, would not be September 3 but September 14. Eleven days had to be taken off the calendar that year because the sun time no longer agreed with calendar time. Only in Britain and the British colonies were people still using the old Julian calendar. For 170 years, all other people of the world had been using the Gregorian calendar. If the British did not change, winter would eventually be coming in July!

Now eleven days had to be knocked off the calendar to agree with the countries using the Gregorian calendar. Some of the boys Tom knew changed their own birthdays to eleven days later. Tom always said his birthday was April 2, O.S., which means "Old Style", but many people claim Tom's birthday is April 13. The change in 1752 also made January 1 the first day of the new year instead of March 25. Some people in England rioted, because they felt eleven days had been taken from their lives.

Tom Jefferson's worst days at school came when he was sick. Luckily for him, he never had any serious illnesses, because the parson's wife had no great knowledge of medicine. Like every wife, she grew herbs in her kitchen garden and stored them to make medicines. Ever since the *Virginia Gazette* had published an article about the miracle cure tar water, she had made each of the boys drink a glass of tar water a day during the seasons when a pestilence was around. But if an ill student did not get better quickly on her camomile tea or soot tea, made with scrapings from the inside of the chimney, she sent for a doctor.

Some, like Dr. Cabell, charged a great deal of money—from one to five pounds just for a visit. For a charge of fifteen pounds, Dr. Cabell guaranteed the patient would live. If he did not live, the patient did not have to pay. In that case, the doctor made his profit from selling one of the coffins he made and having the grave dug.

Most doctors in the colonies had no medical training at all. Anyone could set himself up as a "doctor." When his doctor friend died, Colonel William Byrd of Westover bought his medical bag and a few books. Byrd's medical practice was limited to practicing on his slaves, but even they found him such a bad doctor that they often hid their illnesses from him or ran away rather than try his cures. Bleeding the patient was one of the most common treatments, but no doctor knew how much blood a patient could lose without dying, so the cure was usually much worse than the disease.

The doctor who came to the parsonage used many high-sounding phrases for what ailed the patient, explaining that the bad humours must be brought out at once. To get them out, he induced vomiting, purged his patients with laxatives, sweated them, and finally bled them. He carried an instrument called a scarificator that had a trigger. When he pulled the trigger, tiny blades cut deep enough to draw blood. He put suction cups over the wounds to draw more of the bad-humoured blood out of the body.

One of Tom's fellow students, a boy who had often suffered from sore throats, had a high fever one day. The doctor said his tonsils were filled with bad humours. But no one removed tonsils in those days. Instead, the doctor said he would make the tonsils burst by

applying hot plasters to the throat. He sent some boys out into the barnyard for pigeon and cow dung. He wrapped the fresh hot dung in a piece of torn sheet and pressed it tightly around the boy's throat. No one could pay attention at school that day for listening to their friend's suffering. He was a strong boy and survived the treatment, but many patients did not. When the doctor was leaving, he warned Mrs. Douglass that to prevent the other boys from getting putrified tonsils, she should have each of them bled, either from an arm or foot, about the first days of spring and of fall.

Tom Jefferson watched the slow recovery of his friend. He was not convinced that doctors knew what they were doing. He had heard about Indian medicine men who found medicines that grew naturally in the forest. He wished someone would study the roots and herbs that grew in the colonies and write down the Indian remedies. But he knew the Indians kept their secrets very closely. Learning from them would not be easy.

The disease Americans worried most about was smallpox, and not even the Indians had any cures for it. If a person should be lucky enough to survive the fevers of smallpox, he or she was scarred by ugly pockmarks for life. Some people believed in taking smallpox the "natural way," by visiting someone who had the disease. Young Tom Jefferson read in an encyclopedia that the people of Turkey took their children to visit a person sick with smallpox and actually put some of the poison from a smallpox pustule into an open scratch on their children's arms. He was glad that idea stayed in Turkey. There was no cure or prevention for smallpox in America yet.

8

Indian Secrets

THOMAS Jefferson had waited at the end of the lane for almost an hour before he caught sight of Jupiter and two other slaves from Shadwell. Jupiter spurred his horse and raced ahead.

"We's here, Master Tom!" he shouted. They greeted each other warmly.

The best part of the school year for Tom was this moment when the slaves from Shadwell arrived to take him back home for the summer.

No gentleman in Virginia ever traveled alone on the highway without an escort, and so Tom had no choice but to wait for them to come to Dover Church for him with his horse.

That first summer, returning to Shadwell along the path he had not traveled since he was two years old, Tom could not stop marveling at the beauties of the wild lands. He had lived too long in the crowded Tidewater, where no forests or hills separated the plantations. He remembered that Colonel William Byrd had said Virginia was not named for the Virgin Queen Elizabeth. Byrd said it had been named because it "still retained the Virgin Purity and Plenty of the first Creation." This part of Virginia certainly had Plenty, thought Tom, as he and Jupiter nibbled wild blackberries at nooning. And, drinking his fill from a cold mountain stream, he knew it still had Purity.

Tom Jefferson asked the slaves to tell him when they reached the border of his father's land. His father now owned about 2,500 acres and long before Tom expected it, one of the slaves rode close and pointed.

"Master's land starts at this oak tree, Master Tom."

Tom's mind had been riveted on the fine forests and the blue mountains he could see in the distance. Now his glance moved in the direction of the slave's sweeping hand.

"All that?" he asked. "Even that mountain over there?"

The slaves nodded, pleased that they knew something the young master didn't know. Tom's eyes kept returning to one particular hill that looked treeless on the top. From there he would have quite a view. He determined to climb that small mountain as soon as he had the chance.

The last few miles to Shadwell were the longest. Every sight was new to the ten-year-old. The working part of the plantation now was neatly enclosed by a Virginia worm fence. Virginia fences were made of split rails, usually seven rails high. The rails crossed each other at the ends, and so zigzagged across the fields. Tom chuckled, remembering someone near Dover Church who had drunk too much brandy and could not walk straight.

"He's making a Virginia fence," one of the boys had said.

As soon as they reached Shadwell and Tom Jefferson was surrounded by his family, he wondered how he had ever lived without them so many months. His sister Jane was thirteen and as tall as their mother. Mary, Elizabeth, and Martha all had grown into small ladies. His new little sister Lucy, now almost seven months, beamed at her brother, grasping for a handful of his red hair.

His mother looked a little tired. Life at Shadwell was not as gentle for her as it had been at Tuckahoe, where there were a hundred slaves and several house slaves to do the extra housekeeping jobs. Here there were nowhere near so many slaves and only a few that worked in the house. Jenny Jefferson had to oversee all the household chores.

She took care of the dairy, raised some chickens and geese, and supervised a kitchen garden that, she boasted, could produce thirty different vegetables almost any time of year. She hired a widow to show her daughters how to take apart an old dress and make a new one of the material. When anyone was sick, slave or white, Mrs. Jefferson was both doctor and nurse. Her supply of balms, ointments, salves, potions, and herbs looked like an apothecary shop.

She had slaves making tallow and wax candles and sent men into the forest to bring back candlewood that could be burned for flares in an emergency. She even had a small supply of valuable sperm candles that made a light three times brighter than tallow candles.

Tom was surprised one morning to find his sisters each busily writing down his mother's medical receipts in their handsewn notebooks.

For a Stomachick, Jane wrote carefully, *Stew in brandey ekwal parts of snails, worms, hartshorn shavings and wood sorrel. Seeson with spices and herbs.*

He hurried outdoors to find his father. It was better not to know how their medicines were made.

Peter Jefferson made sure his son had no chance to be soft. He kept him exercising and learning all summer in the fresh air. When the father could take time from his own surveying, he taught his profession to his son. The first place Tom asked to survey was the small mountain he had seen the first day coming home.

Surveyors, Tom learned, had to be very observant. First they took measures and looked over the ground very well. They had to be able to identify every kind of tree and rock. Then they recorded the measurements on a piece of paper, marking down such natural features as a stand of oak trees, ponds, swamps, streams, a granite boulder.

Peter Jefferson showed Tom how to use the surveyor's instruments: theodolite, circumferentor, semicircle, compass, and chain. Large maps were impossible to cope with in the wind, so they plotted the land boundaries on small pieces of paper to transfer onto the large maps later.

The first day they climbed to the top of the little mountain, Tom found it hard to concentrate on surveying. A cool breeze from the west had cleared the sky and the distant blue mountains looked as if he could touch them. In one direction, he could see Shadwell far off and parts of the road. In another, was the gap between the mountains that led to Indian country and the wild West beyond. Now I can imagine what a bird sees, he thought. If only a man could fly.

"I never even imagined it would look like this." Tom spoke slowly because, to his surprise, he was having trouble swallowing a lump from his throat. Words rushed into his mind, and he could not use any of them to speak. Tom was never to find another spot on earth that affected him in the same way the little mountain could.

Peter Jefferson taught his son to shoot that first summer back at Shadwell. He made the boy practice lifting the heavy gun, supporting it along the barrel with his left arm, and then pulling the trigger. Next he allowed Tom some powder, but no shot, until he learned not to flinch at the loud explosion. At last he allowed him to use shot, warning that the homemade shot was not to be wasted.

"If you hit a tree, take your penknife and dig the shot out. Not one ball can be wasted."

Tom practiced many hours, just as he had with his violin, until he was sure of his skill. Then one day his father sent him off on his own to shoot something for dinner.

"Bring home anything," he told his ten-year-old son, "But please remember, you don't shoot a squirrel smack in the middle because there won't be anything left of it to make a pie from."

He showed Tom how to "bark" a squirrel by aiming between the animal and the tree bark.

"And never pursue a small animal until it's too tired or scared before it dies. If you do, too much lactic acid gets into its system and its meat spoils faster. Kill it while it's moving. And aim well in front."

Tom went off trying to remember all that a hunter needed to know and certain in his heart he would return with their family dinner. But the day was long and he never even saw anything to shoot at. He flopped exhausted under a tree and listened for rabbit sounds. What he heard sounded very like a turkey gobble. Stalking as quietly as he knew how, Tom followed the sound and in a small clearing saw a good sized turkey . . . in a homemade cage! One of the slaves had been fattening it in the woods for his own family.

Tom could not shoot the turkey while it was caged. So he took one of his garters, tied it around the turkey's leg, and fastened it to a tree so it couldn't get away. Then he shot it. When Tom returned home, dragging his turkey, he had grown ten feet tall in the eyes of his mother and sisters. His father, knowing very well that a couple of turkeys had been missing from the poultry yard, let Tom have his day of glory.

Some days Peter Jefferson showed his son how to survive in the wilds the Indian way. He showed him how to crush the leaves of the mullein or fishweed plant or the seeds of the southern buckeye and to scatter them on a pond where the water was still. Suddenly a fish rose to the surface and floated as if it were asleep.

"It's a narcotic," his father told Tom. "The fish is drugged, but only for a short while. Reach down and put your hand around it."

Tom was sure it would dart out of his grasp, but it lay as gently as a tame cat. A second later it leaped into the water and swam quickly into the deep. He hadn't wanted to kill it, but he liked knowing he could catch something to eat if he were ever lost in the forest.

"Did Ontasseté show you how to do that?" he asked, proud that his father was good friends with the Cherokee wise man. "Why do the Indians know so many secrets they won't tell white men?"

"They do tell us," said his father. "But sometimes white people aren't listening. We ask how they shave off their face hair and they laugh at us. The truth is that Indians have very little facial hair, but Englishmen who never knew any Indians refuse to believe that. They keep asking Indians what magic preparation they use to shave. A few years ago, while we were living at Tuckahoe, some Indians even conjured up a rainstorm over Colonel Byrd's plantation during a drought. When Colonel Byrd told his friends in Williamsburg about his rain shower, which he paid for with two bottles of rum, his friends didn't believe him. Indians live so close to nature that some of their feats do seem like magic to us."

The summer Tom was eleven, his father took him deer hunting in the Indian manner.

"Now try to think like an Indian," he warned. "You must be very quiet and extremely patient."

When they were near the hunting place, they dismounted and took their saddles off their horses. Both hunters wore Indian moccasins. For an hour, it seemed to Tom, they walked the horses through the forest, letting the animals set the pace.

The horses roamed casually through the underbrush, sniffing here and taking a leaf from a branch there. Bent half over beside his meandering horse so a deer wouldn't see him, Tom felt as if every muscle in his body was trying to scream. At last, peeking around his horse, he spotted a deer grazing with her fawn. The deer saw and smelled only the horse and calmly continued grazing. They were close enough to shoot the deer easily, when suddenly some

second sense warned her. In an instant, both doe and fawn took off through the brush.

Every summer, as soon as Tom returned from school at the parsonage of the Reverend Douglass, he went to the little mountain. Tom liked the other pupils at his school, and he loved his noisy sisters at home, but sometimes a man had to have a place where he could lie down, stare at the clouds, and just think. The little mountain supplied a need in Tom's life that not even Shadwell gave him.

Young Thomas often brightened the family evenings with his violin, and Jane taught them some of her happy songs. He was the man of the house during the long summer weeks when his father was away from home working with Joshua Fry on the Virginia border map. When they completed the job at last, they made several copies before they trusted the map to a ship bound for England, where it was printed. The first copies of the new map were sold in Williamsburg in April 1755.

Social life at Shadwell was not as exciting as it had been at Tuckahoe. Small stores had now opened along the Three-Notched Road and the road that ran northward. The shops of Thomas Meriwether, Robert and David Lewis, and Thomas Walker were beginning to make the road junction look like a tiny town. Several mills appeared on the streams that ran down to the James River. Joel Terrell opened an "ordinary" or tavern on the Three-Notched Road, where he charged one shilling for a meal and four pence to sleep in a bed, but seven pence to stable a horse.

Tom heard all about the fair in the next county, but he probably was not encouraged to make the trip. Fairs attracted a wild crowd, said his mother. There were always quarter races and gamblers to collect money from the losing bets, and there was cudgeling and boxing, bloody sports for a boy to watch.

Visitors came to Shadwell constantly. Tom enjoyed hearing Dr. Thomas Walker tell about his adventures. In 1750 he had led a party of explorers into the backcountry of Virginia through a break in the mountains called Cumberland Gap. Even though the group had traveled for days, they still had not reached the great Mississippi River, which everyone knew was the western border of Virginia. Tom Jefferson never tired of stories about exploring in the West.

Another visitor Tom enjoyed was his friend Dabney Carr. Dabney was his own age, but they saw each other only in summer, because Dabney went to the Reverend Maury's school near Shadwell.

Ever since Tom's first look at his father's map of Virginia, he had wanted to see the Indian burial mound that was marked on it. His father had warned him not to go near the mound, for it was sacred ground to the Indians.

"What harm can come of it?" Tom said to Dabney early one morning when they were riding west. "The Monacan Indians have not even lived around here for at least sixty years."

No harm at all, Dabney agreed. He was always ready for any adventure Tom suggested.

There had once been Indian villages in the area around the Rivanna River valley. Tom and Dabney often picked up pottery fragments, pieces of quartzite, and once a grooved stone that could have been an ax head. These treasures they put away carefully for the "philosophy cabinet" they would start some day. But this day Tom led Dabney northward toward the place where the Rivanna came out of the mountains.

They stopped to noon in a clearing by the river with wild berries for dessert.

"I think we should leave our horses here and walk the rest of the way," Tom suggested. He would not admit to Dabney that the tales he had heard of trespassing on sacred Indian ground were beginning to haunt him. Instead, he said, "This is Mr. Moorman's land, and I don't want him to know we are here."

Dabney tried to avoid stepping on a twig and plunged noisily into a dead branch on the ground. Tom shushed him when he tried to say "Sorry."

They walked almost an hour, staying along the Rivanna riverbed to a point where it curved toward the west. Tom pointed silently. Somehow the place did not strike either of them as a spot in which to talk loudly.

The mound appeared before them, like a twelve-foot high hill with a flat top. Large trees that had evidently been there many years grew out of the top. Around the base, the boys could see where the Indians had dug out a hollow about five feet deep to get the soil for the mound. They were just about to approach when some instinct warned Tom not to move. He snatched at Dabney's shirt sleeve and held on tight. They inched back behind a bush, Tom holding a finger to his lips.

Coming straight out of the woods toward them was a party of Indians. They rode slowly, single file, on horseback. The leader, a very old man, turned his horse to face the mound and the others followed. For at least fifteen minutes they sat there in dead silence, the only sound the swishing of their horses' tails. Then, just as silently as they had arrived, the Indians turned their horses and rode back into the dense forest. Once Dabney shifted his weight to the other knee and a twig snapped. But if the Indians heard, they never turned to look.

For a long time neither boy dared to speak. They had been walking quietly back toward their horses for several minutes before Dabney whispered, "What kind of Indians were they?"

"I've no idea," said Tom. "But I heard Mr. Moorman say he'd seen Indians here before. He said they just follow an unseen path about six miles through the woods, never asking anyone where the grave is, and then return to wherever they came from."

"Sure is spooky," said Dabney.

"I do wish we'd had a chance to dig there," said Tom. "But after seeing the Indians, looking so sorrowful and quiet, I don't feel right disturbing the graves anyway. I'm going back someday, though, when I know just how to dig in the mound, so we can learn something about the Indians' history."

Tom's father became a burgess for Albemarle County in 1754. Now he made four journeys a year to Williamsburg during the public times to meet with the other burgesses at the capitol. He also became a justice of the peace, and people streamed up the hill to Shadwell so that he could settle their grievances. Peter Jefferson was also made county lieutenant in charge of the militia. Since the death of General Braddock, during the fighting against the French and Indians in Pennsylvania, the settlers near the mountains had more cause to worry about Indians. Many men now volunteered for the militia, but wanted to stay nearby and defend their own homes. As if to top a year already filled with news, Jenny Jefferson had twins in October 1755, a girl named Anne and a boy, Randolph.

When fourteen-year-old Tom Jefferson rode home to Shadwell the summer of 1757, he knew it was the end of his schooling at Dover Church. The price of tobacco had gone down and the Reverend Douglass was not making enough money. He moved his family to Monrovia plantation to teach the children of Colonel

Spence Monroe. (Monroe's son James, born the following year and taught by Douglass, was to become the fifth president of the United States.) Tom knew he needed more reading in Latin and Greek. He planned to ask his father to send him to Reverend Maury's school.

The summer passed quickly. Peter Jefferson was often away, and when he was home he seemed unwell. Tom couldn't imagine his father sick. The slaves still talked about the time down at the docks when two slaves had complained about the heavy hogsheads of tobacco they had to lift.

"I never ask any man to do work that I could not do myself," Peter Jefferson said. He walked down the dock and grabbed up one hogshead. Then, while he held it, he slowly raised the second one from the dock. All the slaves cheered, and loyal feeling for their master was always strong after that. Another time, when two slaves were having trouble pushing down a rickety outbuilding, Peter Jefferson tied a rope around it, gave a mighty heave, and the shed collapsed in a heap of boards.

Tom's sisters took a new interest in him that summer he was growing so much taller. Jane and Mary were both attracting boys. Now they found in their brother a male person with whom they could speak frankly. For Mary, Tom was someone to consult about hair styles and becoming dress colors. She loved to dance with him and respected his opinions about the boys she knew.

But to Jane, Tom was someone who would listen to her secret longings. One day, when he teased her about being old enough to marry, he was surprised that she did not go all soft and giggly like Mary.

"You're seventeen," he said, "and our mother was only sixteen when she and Father married."

"Do you realize, little brother," Jane replied, "that if I marry I will lose all my identity? My husband can dictate to me even whether I can cut my hair or pull a hair from my eyebrows! These men expect to own a girl, like a slave," she complained.

Tom had to admit it was true. A woman had no rights at all. She belonged to her husband. She did not even own the clothes on her back. Jane was a bright educated girl, yet her husband could forbid her to read the books on his library shelf.

"Even my children would not be mine, but his," she went on. "And that's another thing. Our mother is exhausted from having babies. I feel as if I've already raised a brother and four sisters, and now there are the twins. The last thing in the world I want right now is a houseful of my own children."

"But, Jane, that's the way things are supposed to be," said Tom. "Women are supposed to have children. That's what they're made for, isn't it?"

"Why? Why can't women go to school and learn Latin? I can read your first Latin book. Why can't I be a teacher?"

Tom felt he was walking on thin ice. If he told Jane that a woman's brain is more delicate than a man's and not capable of serious study, she might explode. Nor would she care to hear the opinion of the Reverend Douglass that the Bible tells women they should just have children. Jane was too smart for the ordinary answers that men gave women.

"You'll feel different when you meet someone you love," he said lamely.

Jane gave him a withering look that could have ended their first argument. But just then Jupiter came running from the direction of the house.

"Master Tom, Miss Jane, come quick! Master Jefferson's done got sick and he looks like to die."

9

Tall Thomas Alone

"I'm alone . . . all alone." The words kept going through Thomas Jefferson's mind, and yet he knew they were not true. He was far from alone, with a mother, six sisters, and a brother. But the alone feeling did not go away.

Peter Jefferson died on August 17, 1757. Dr. Walker had come immediately and hardly left his bedside for two days.

"It shouldn't have happened," he told the family. "Peter has always been so strong."

But it *had* happened, and somehow Thomas had to learn to deal with it. He had watched something go out of his mother's eyes that he knew he would never see again. The girls all turned to him for comfort. He wondered if anything he said could possibly help them.

Thomas sent riders to other plantations as far away as Williamsburg to "give the invitations" to come to the funeral. Rarely did anyone refuse such an invitation. Attending a person's funeral was the last duty one could pay to a fellow human.

Jenny went to the kitchen house to tell the cook that funeral cakes must be baked and wine chilled. The family plunged into the preparations that had to be made for guests who traveled many miles to the funeral.

It's almost as if we were giving a party, Tom thought with distaste. But by the week's end, he realized the hard work had kept them all so busy that the first difficult days had hurried past.

The reading of the will hurt most. Peter Jefferson had left Thomas his most cherished possessions—his books, the mathematical instruments Tom had learned to survey with, his "Cherry Tree Desk and Bookcase," and his trusted mulatto slave Sawney. Shadwell was to be Jenny's while she lived. Tom was to have the little mountain, and there was land for two-year-old Randolph in case he lived to be twenty-one. Peter instructed Tom to save a wedding gift of two hundred pounds for each of the girls.

Most valuable of all to Tom was his father's leaving money and orders to continue his education. Four friends were to advise Tom until he reached the age of twenty-one himself. And Peter had added one gentle reminder to his son: always take plenty of exercise.

Tom fled several times to his little mountain to roam quietly through the forest and view the rest of the world from its summit. He always came home feeling better, but he never lost the lonely feeling that he had hoped would go away.

One day at the little mountain, Tom Jefferson discovered that he was not alone. A twig snapped not far from where he lay flat on his back watching the clouds change shape. For the first time in a long while, he laughed.

"That's no Indian coming," he said without turning over. "How did you find me, Dab?"

"Easy. You've been coming here a lot lately," said his friend. "I just thought this time you might want company."

Tom was surprised to discover that Dabney was right. It felt good just to talk. Before an hour had passed, the two boys were roaming across the top of the mountain, planning where a house should be built.

"Here's a good place for the stables." Dabney pointed.

"That's the worst place I can imagine," said Tom. "Don't you feel the wind here? My whole house would smell just like the stables. The hottest day in summer there's a breeze at this spot. I think I'll build a tunnel from here to the basement. That way I can make the breeze blow inside."

They plotted the garden on the sunny southern slope and out-buildings somewhere out of sight of the house. Tom discovered he had many more ideas about building a house.

"How about putting the kitchen and stables and some of the other ugly buildings under the ground?" he asked Dabney.

"What? You can't do that!"

"Why not?"

"It's never been done," Dabney insisted.

"A lot of things have never been done," said Tom. "Maybe it's time to stop doing things the way they have always been done. You know General Braddock was killed because he insisted on fighting Indians the way the British have always fought. You couldn't even hunt a deer in the forest wearing a bright red uniform. If Braddock had dressed his men in forest colors like the Indians, a lot fewer soldiers would have died this year."

They had roamed to the shade of a huge old oak tree just downhill from the imaginary house.

"It's so cool here," said Dabney. "I'd like to be buried here." He could have bitten off his tongue for bringing up the subject. But Tom had let go of his morbid thoughts.

"So would I," he agreed. "Let's promise each other that whoever dies first, the other one will bury him here."

That fall Thomas began lessons with the Reverend James Maury, who kept a school at the foot of the Southwest Mountains, not far from Shadwell. Maury was a Huguenot and had lived in Man-akin town. He had a small farm of 400 acres at Fredericksville parish and a dozen children. He had become an Anglican preacher, but now, with prices going down, his payment of 16,000 pounds of tobacco brought him only half enough money to feed them all.

Luckily, Maury owned a library of four hundred books and was a gifted teacher. He opened a school in an area where one was badly needed. A year of school and board cost Thomas Jefferson 20 pounds sterling. For this he learned the classics, manners and morals, literature, grammar, history, geography, and mathematics. Children in the lower school learned only reading, writing, and arithmetic, and they paid only 15 shillings.

Maury had so many dislikes, it was a wonder he could teach at all. He found the Scots who lived in the hills "raw and surly." He could see no good in the many small churches of new religions that were springing up wherever immigrants settled. All Indians he called barbarians. The rest of mankind who did not agree with him were classified as "the vulgar herd."

Thomas had four other students in his class: his friend Dabney Carr, William James Madison, who grew up to be President of William and Mary College and whose cousin was fourth President of the United States; James Maury, a son of the teacher; and John Walker at whose wedding, some years later, Tom was a groomsman.

"I'm glad I didn't come to this school any sooner," Thomas told Dabney one Sunday evening after the last church service had ended. "I'd have had my religion ruined completely."

Reverend Maury bombarded the boys with dire warnings that they were not prepared for eternity at all. All their enjoyments, he said, and everything they owned were tempting them to evil ways. They were only thinking of having a good time when their lives should be spent preparing for death.

As often as he could, Tom escaped to Shadwell and the pleasures he shared with his family. After a hard week with the Reverend Maury, playing the violin as Jane sang soothed his jangled feelings.

"The parson's a good classical teacher," he told the family. "I'm learning what I need to know to get into college."

One thing Tom Jefferson's friends could never understand about him—he loved studying. Many years later, his friend James Maury said, "Even when we had an unexpected holiday from school, Tom always prepared the next day's lesson first and then went out to have fun."

Fun for Tom was to pick up his gun and head for the hills. He usually came back with something for dinner, a welcome gift for the many mouths Mrs. Maury had to feed. Often his hunting trips were close enough to Shadwell so that he could carry home food for his own family.

Shadwell plantation was running smoothly under a good overseer who was allowed to keep one seventh of the earnings. The tobacco crop was now close to five thousand pounds and improving every year. Expenses for running the plantation came to 30 pounds a year and the tobacco brought in 48 pounds.

Toward the end of 1759, Jefferson found he was spending more time at Shadwell than at school. As master of the plantation, he could not walk out to go to school when important visitors came. Some of the visitors stayed many weeks at a time "to help the poor widow with all her children." A maiden aunt moved in to help with sewing, and a childhood friend of Jenny's came to stay. Tom dreaded the battle he saw ahead, but some of the visitors had to go. There would not be enough food for his own family if they did not leave.

That Christmas season Thomas Jefferson went to visit one of his guardians, Colonel Peter Randolph, who lived at Chatsworth plantation on the James River. Tom's violin and the lively music he played made him a popular guest at parties. But Colonel Randolph had the young man's nonmusical future in mind when he called him into his office to talk about college.

"Money spent on your education is never wasted," said Colonel Randolph. "Write to John Harvie as soon as you get back home. He controls the purse strings."

Thomas's mind was reeling with hope all the way back to Shadwell. He worded the letter over and over as his horse trotted along the frozen mud path. Harvie was a careful man with money. Tom would somehow have to convince him it would save money if he went to college. But how? He wrote the letter in his mind five hundred times over before he finally sat down with quill in hand.

Shadwell, Jan. 14, 1760

Sir,

  I was at Colo. Peter Randolph's about a Fortnight ago, and my Schooling falling into Discourse, he said he thought it would be to my Advantage to go to the College, and was desirous I should go, as indeed I am myself for several Reasons. In the first place as long as I stay at the Mountains the Loss of one fourth of my Time is inevitable, by Company's coming here and detaining me from School. And likewise my Absence will in a great Measure put a Stop to so much Company, and by that Means lessen the Expences of the Estate in House-Keeping. And on the other Hand by going to the College I shall get a more universal Acquaintance, which may hereafter be serviceable to me; and I suppose I can pursue my Studies in the Greek and Latin as well there as here, and likewise learn something of the Mathematics. I shall be glad of your opinion.

10

Williamsburg Days

THOMAS Jefferson had never seen a city when he and Jupiter rode into Williamsburg a few weeks before his seventeenth birthday.

In the bustling activity of the public times, few people noticed the tall gangling redhead and his manservant. Tom asked the way to the college and found he had already ridden past it.

The College of William and Mary was not new. It had begun in 1693 as a school to educate Indian boys. So far it had not succeeded with the Indians, and in March of 1760, when Tom arrived, it did not have a very good reputation. The college had three large buildings that Tom found hideous.

"The college buildings," he told Jane, "look like a rude, misshapen pile which, except for the fact they have roofs, might be mistaken for brick kilns."

One of the brick piles was a grammar school "for boys who had never learned Latin." Tom thought it degrading to have a school for children included in the college grounds.

A second brick pile was Brafferton Hall, which housed only a few Indian students by then. Going to school did not appeal to Indians, and the experiment to turn them into civilized Christian Englishmen was beginning to look like a big failure. The few Indian boys who stuck it out because they had been sent to represent their tribes could hardly wait for the day when they could peel off their hated English clothes, change into Indian garb, and ride off into the hills free men again.

The third was the college building. Three professors made up the entire faculty. One taught the boys who wanted to be ministers.

A second professor taught scientific subjects, and a third taught whatever subjects were left over.

Tom had plenty of time to look over Williamsburg. He was not admitted as a student until two weeks after his arrival. The reason

may have been that the college's terms were divided, as they were in England, into Lent term, beginning January 14, Easter term, Trinity term, and Michaelmas. Thomas must have arrived before Easter term began.

Professors came and went so fast that the students hardly knew who would sit in front of the class the next day. Many professors were thrown out for heavy drinking and card playing in the taverns of Williamsburg.

Tom's first professor of moral philosophy was the Reverend Jacob Rowe. He was thrown out for carousing and leading the students in a battle against the town boys. The college president, Thomas Dawson, looked around for a replacement and found a man visiting from England. He was a talented mathematics professor. For Thomas Jefferson, Dawson could not have found a better teacher.

Professor William Small stayed only four years at the college, but he came just when young Tom was ripe for learning. He knew how to inspire a young man who was afraid he had no future because he was not a good orator. Professor Small was often criticized, especially by the divinity professor, for encouraging his students to think for themselves instead of thinking as the Church of England taught them to think. But Small believed in freedom in learning as well as freedom in religion.

Jefferson lived at the college, probably having a small bedroom to himself that opened onto one large room he shared with three or four other boys. Jupiter bunked near Tom so that he could be within calling distance. The horses were sent back to the country until they were needed again at the end of the semester for riding home.

The first night in his room, Tom wondered what his roommates were like. They had gone for a night on the town and never came in until morning. Tom had just come back from his morning run through Williamsburg and was soaking his feet in cold water when they burst through the door.

"Look who's here," shouted the first. Tom stood up, his feet making wet puddles on the bare floor, which Jupiter tried vainly to wipe up.

"I'm John Page," said the second. "Welcome to Devilsburgh, Mr. Thomas Jefferson. He's Francis Willis." He waved toward the other.

"Pleased to make your acquaintance, Tall Tom," said Willis, so seriously that Tom was not sure whether he was being teased or accepted. His face turned a bright red, but the two were so friendly that he soon relaxed. A third boy had been expelled for a couple of weeks for fighting with a town boy.

"He's rusticating," said Willis.

"That means he went to the country," Page explained. "We're not allowed to go into town alone, because there has been some trouble. So we all go together."

Jefferson had not known there was a rule about going into town. Every morning for two years now he had taken an early morning run, followed by a cold foot bath, to prevent colds and fevers. He decided that on the days when he rose early enough to avoid being caught, he would run through the town. Otherwise his early runs would be out toward the country.

He was surprised by how quickly he became accustomed to the routine of college life and how very much he enjoyed his new friends.

A Virginia boy who wanted to go to college had very few choices, not because college was hard to get into, but because there were so few of them. Colleges in New England were generally ruled out because they were so far away, and the fun-loving Virginians had heard too many tales about stern New Englanders. That left New Jersey College at Princeton, full of Presbyterians, and the College of Philadelphia, later called the University of Pennsylvania. There was not a single medical school or law school in the colonies. The College of William and Mary had one great advantage. It was in Virginia.

Sundays, the students were supposed to attend services in the chapel in the south wing of the college building. But Jefferson soon learned that almost any activity was preferred to chapel-going.

When Thomas Jefferson grew up, he said his college days were passed "in dull monotony of colonial subservience." By then he had forgotten, or thought he had better not mention, some of the less dull and monotonous things he had done. His first year was almost his undoing.

His roommates, especially Francis Willis of Gloucester, who was a gay blade, kept Jefferson from poring over his books too often. Sometimes Tom started the evening with his friends. Then suddenly, when they had just begun to celebrate, he would politely excuse himself and go back to his books. Inside his head he could hear old Reverend Maury's dire warnings: "Flee from the enchantress Pleasure! When you are most inclined to stay for another bottle, that's the sure time to go."

One night, when Jefferson had left his friends to study, his roommates came back to the room late. The sight of Tom studying hard touched a fuse in Willis. He overturned the desk, knocked over the candle lamp, snatched Tom's books and ran. But Willis was no match for Jefferson, whose morning runs had put him in

very good condition. John Page had to step in before the two boys were accused of fighting and sent off for three weeks to "rusticate."

Five students invited Jefferson to join what they called the F.H.C. Society. The group of six youths formed the first college fraternity in the New World. What the letters F.H.C. stood for was never revealed by any of its members. The boys who were not asked to join called them the Flat Hat Club. Each member wore a medal stamped with F.H.C. on one side, clasped hands and a motto on the other. They wore their medals on their pocket watch guards, where they were easily noticed. Of course this meant Jefferson had

to buy a fancy watch—a luxury he would never have allowed himself back at Shadwell.

He permitted himself other luxuries as well: shiny new dancing pumps, an embroidered vest, and handsome city clothes. He tried everything: plays, dances, card playing, horse racing, fox hunting. It was almost as if he were trying to get his years at parsons' schools out of his blood.

Thomas felt so guilty that, at the end of the year, he told his guardian John Harvie to charge him for the expenses.

"It's not fair to take my expenses from the money that goes to my sisters and brother," he said.

Jefferson enjoyed living high for a while, but after a few months of it, Professor Small decided Thomas had had enough.

"I'd like you to bring your violin and meet a friend of mine," he said one evening the first summer. The "friend" turned out to be no less a personage than Lieutenant Governor Francis Fauquier. After one evening of playing chamber music with the lieutenant governor and his friends, Tom's eyes were opened. This was living high—not the carousing of college boys. He went once a week to the Governor's Palace.

Professor Small introduced him to George Wythe, a lawyer. Wythe took Jefferson for his first look at a court of English law. Thomas felt uncomfortable when the prisoner was led into court in chains.

"Prisoner, thou are indicted by the name of John Taylor for the felony of theft. How sayest thou, guilty or not guilty?"

The prisoner whispered, "Not guilty," and the clerk said, "Culprit, how wilt thou be tried?" This question once had three answers, "by combat, by ordeal, or by jury," but now there was only trial by jury, so the proper answer they had told the prisoner, was "By God and my country."

A jury was then sworn in. Jefferson asked Wythe how the jury could possibly be impartial when every one of them knew all about the crime before it had been tried in court.

"The jury is especially chosen from where the crime occurred so they know about the matter," George Wythe answered. He cast a sideways glance at the redhead. The boy shows a good mind, he thought. He's right. The jury cannot possibly be impartial.

After hearing the testimony, the jury was ready to announce the verdict. Jefferson relaxed for the first time when he heard it.

"Not guilty." The prisoner was told to fall on his knees and thank the jury. He was lucky, thought Tom. If he had been convicted of highway robbery, a far worse crime than robbery on a city street, he would have been hanged.

Before the end of Jefferson's second college year, George Wythe had invited him to study law and help him with his legal practice.

One day in 1762, Thomas noticed much excitement among the Indian students at Brafferton Hall.

"Ontasseté speaks the night of the full moon," one of the Indian boys explained to Tom. Ontasseté, now the Cherokee tribe's most loved orator, was among the Indians chosen to sail to London and be presented to the white man's new king, George III. The Indians hoped to show the English ruler that Indians also had noble leaders. Ontasseté's speech near Williamsburg was to ask for safety on the voyage and for the safety of his people while he was away.

On the night of the full moon, Jefferson and several friends walked the few miles to the encampment. Some of the tribal elders recognized the red-haired son of Peter Jefferson and nodded solemnly. While Ontasseté spoke, addressing himself to the moon, not a sound was heard but the crackling of Indian campfires. Every eye was glued on the speaker. His spell stayed with the boys all the way back to the college. Most of Tom's friends had never seen an Indian encampment or so many Indians at once. Yet the main thought of each boy was that they had heard a gifted speaker— even though not one word had been spoken in a language they understood.

"I wonder whether our king will be as deeply impressed as we were," Thomas murmured. He knew a wealthy Virginian could be made to feel small and unimportant by English nobles dressed in ermine, velvets, satins, and gold jewelry. He hoped that this noble man would not be hurt.

Now that Jefferson was in college, his trips back and forth to Shadwell took four times as long. He was invited to visit several days at the plantations of his new friends and with uncles and cousins he had never known well. Because he was often asked to play his violin at parties, he always carried pages of the newest music he could find at the Williamsburg bookstore. The shy redhead was popular with the young women as well as with the men.

At one party he met Patrick Henry. They became friends at once, because they both loved music. But in no way were they alike. While Tom Jefferson studied law for years to learn every twist and turn, Patrick Henry breezed through enough reading in six weeks to pass his bar exams and began collecting fees for practicing law. The law professor, George Wythe, was shocked, but Tom knew how Patrick hated to study. What Tom admired most in him was his gift for speaking, a talent that Tom knew would never be his.

Tom liked girls—all of them. The warnings that all women were "Syrens" fell on deaf ears. One night at a ball, a college friend, Lewis Burwell, Jr., introduced his sister Rebecca to Tom.

Tom made all the gentlemanly motions, bowed and kissed her hand, but hardly a word could he utter. He stood there, just as he had at age five in front of his first tutor, muttering a few broken sentences and wishing the floor would open up and swallow him. What impression Thomas Jefferson made on the beautiful Rebecca is lost to history. But Tom plunged headlong in love. He carried her picture inside his watch case and dreamed of the words he would whisper to her.

One summer day when he was nineteen, Jefferson was visiting John Page at Rosewell in Gloucester County.

"She's just over that piece of water." Tom waved toward the York River. Rebecca Burwell lived with her guardian in the town of York.

"If only we had a neat little sloop," John moaned.

"Wait," Tom cried. "A sloop is too good. We'll rig that tobacco flat and sail over with it. She's bound to invite us to spend the night if we don't have a safe-looking boat!"

John and Tom worked for hours rigging the clumsy flatboat. They waited for slack tide before trying to cross the wide river. Even then the barge moved like a heavy log raft. As they maneuvered it into the creek, hopping in the water to shove it off sand bars, Tom began to waver.

"What if she's angry?" he worried.

"She should be delighted. We've come to save her from the pirates," John argued.

The lovely Miss Burwell came running out on the lawn with her sister, and it was too late to back off. She was not angry, but quite pleased. Tom never said all the words he wanted to say to her. But John seemed to say enough for both of them. Tom was content just to stand by her side and feel her gentle breath on his arm.

Sailing their ungainly craft back by moonlight, Tom was able to tell John all the words he had wanted to say to the fair "Belinda," as he called her. Why, then, couldn't he have spoken the right words to her face?

Thomas Jefferson left college that year. He had decided to study law with George Wythe. But, he argued, he could learn law far better back at Shadwell, if Wythe would give him a list of the books to be read and tell him what order to read them in.

As Thomas rode off, a year's supply of lawbooks packed in his trunk, a few of the professors and students may have wondered about the lanky redhead. Was he just another half-educated man? They were sure he would never be much of a public speaker, but they also thought that if Thomas Jefferson said he was going to become a lawyer, then he would be one. Only Professor William Small knew in his heart that this young man had something very special to give to the world. Unhappily the professor did not live long enough to find out what that special something was.

Thomas Jefferson became a lawyer five years later, but he never did express himself well by speaking. Although he tried a few more times, he was never even able to speak about love to Rebecca Burwell. She married another man shortly after Thomas left college.

Jefferson found that his great strength was with written words. In 1769 he was elected to the House of Burgesses and worked to change some of Virginia's outdated laws. No longer would the rich plantation owners run the government to suit themselves. Jefferson separated the government from the Church of England, and soon

Virginians no longer had to support the state church. He also ended the practice of leaving huge estates to only the eldest son, a system that kept the plantations from ever being divided up into smaller plots of land.

In 1775 Thomas was chosen as one of the Virginia delegates to attend the Second Continental Congress in Philadelphia. The next year one of the Virginians, Richard Henry Lee, proposed that "these United Colonies are, and of right ought to be, free and independent States." The men asked Thomas to help put Lee's speech into written words. Within three weeks, Thomas Jefferson had written down on paper the Declaration of Independence.

Later, when Jefferson was Governor of Virginia, he served on the board at the College of William and Mary. The school became the first university in America to have an elective system of studies, so a young man could learn a number of professions, and to begin a school to teach law.

Thomas Jefferson had married a young widow, Martha Wayles Skelton, in 1772. At last he built his house on the little mountain and named it Monticello, which means "little mountain" in Italian. His wife Martha lived only ten years and left him with three little girls. The youngest died soon after her mother, but Martha, called "Patty," and Maria, called "Polly," grew up, married, and gave Thomas many grandchildren to love.

The tiny village near the Rivanna Water Gap had by then become a city named Charlottesville. There, within sight of Monticello, Jefferson founded the University of Virginia. Ever since it opened in 1825 its students have called it "Thomas Jefferson University."

Looking back over his life when he was old and most of his friends were gone, Thomas Jefferson amused himself one day by designing his own tombstone to be placed under the oak tree at Monticello.

"I want the following inscription—and not a word more," he stated.

Here was buried
Thomas Jefferson
Author of the Declaration of Independence
Of the Statute of Virginia for religious freedom
& Father of the University of Virginia

Whatever Happened To . . . ?

CARR, DABNEY. Tom Jefferson's friend Dabney married Tom's younger sister Martha in 1765. After he died, Thomas asked Martha and her six children to move in with him at Monticello. Dabney is buried under the oak tree just as Tom promised.

COLLEGE OF WILLIAM AND MARY. The F.H.C. Society became an honorary fraternity called Phi Beta Kappa in 1776. Besides being the first fraternity on an American campus, its members are among the best scholars in the country.

When Jefferson was Governor of Virginia in 1779 and a member of the college board, the grammar school and the divinity school were closed. Under Jefferson's guidance, the university began courses in anatomy, medicine, law, police studies, and modern languages.

JEFFERSON, ANNE SCOTT. One of the twins, she married Hastings Marks.

JEFFERSON, JANE. Tom's favorite sister never married. She died at Shadwell, age twenty-five, possibly of smallpox. Letters Tom wrote at that time indicated a smallpox epidemic in Virginia. Also, the following spring, he traveled north to Philadelphia to "receive the smallpox" under a doctor's care. This was considered important before a man married, to lessen his chances of dying from the disease after he had several children dependent on him.

JEFFERSON, JENNY (Jane Randolph). Tom's mother lived at Shadwell until the end of March 1776. In this story, she has been called "Jenny," the nickname in those days for Jane, to distinguish her from Tom's sister Jane.

JEFFERSON, LUCY. Tom's little sister Lucy married Charles Lilburn Lewis.

JEFFERSON, MARTHA. Tom's younger sister Martha married Dabney Carr. After Carr died, she lived for a while at Monticello with their six children.

JEFFERSON, MARY. Tom's sister Mary married Thomas Bolling in 1760. Tom visited often at their home, "Fairfields," in Chesterfield County.

JEFFERSON, RANDOLPH. Tom's little brother, the other twin, married Anne Lewis and moved to Fluvanna County on the land left to him by his father when he was two.

JEFFERSON, THOMAS. See THOMAS JEFFERSON, THE MAN, following.

JUPITER. Tom's slave, who was exactly his age, became his coachman in later years. Jupiter died several months before Jefferson became President of the United States in the 1800 election. Even though ill, Jupiter had insisted on making the trip to Philadelphia with Jefferson and died after nine days of illness. "His death," said Thomas, "leaves a void in my administration which I cannot fill up."

LITTLE MOUNTAIN. Tom Jefferson's favorite spot in the world became his home when he started building there about 1770. He used the Italian word for "little mountain" and called it Monticello.

Nowhere in America can you visit a place that shows more of the personality of its builder. Jefferson's greatest pleasure came in thinking up new things for Monticello. He invented storm windows for wintry days on the mountain, a revolving writing chair, a music stand four players could use at the same time, and a dumbwaiter to lift his wine bottles straight from the basement to the side of his dining room mantel. An automatic clock, still working after more than 150 years, tells not only the hour but the day of the week. He wrote a dictionary of Indian dialects, and the many books he collected at Monticello were the start of the Library of Congress. His bedroom had a circular clothes hanger, and his bed was in the wall between two rooms; he had only to get out of one side to be in his study or the other to be in his dressing room. A visitor to Monticello can see all these inventions today.

RANDOLPH, THOMAS MANN. Evidently Thomas Mann also grew up loving a large close family, since he had thirteen children. One, Thomas Mann Randolph, Jr., married Thomas Jefferson's daughter, Martha Jefferson.

RICHMOND. The town laid out in 1740 by Colonel William Byrd was not a failure after all. The days of large plantations that were inherited intact by elder sons were coming to an end. Jefferson saw Richmond growing while he was at college in Williamsburg.

In 1779 the capitol of Virginia was moved there from Williamsburg. Although the town was burned to the ground by Benedict Arnold during the Revolution, it was rebuilt in 1782 and has been growing ever since.

SHADWELL. The house built by Peter Jefferson burned down in 1770 but was rebuilt. Thomas declared he would rather have lost his money than the family treasures he lost that day. Today Shadwell is marked only by a historical marker along a back road, easily missed by tourists who cling to the Interstate highway. Looking up its entrance drive across the locked fence, you can see a row of trees. Tom followed the custom that a young master in Virginia planted a row of trees on his twenty-first birthday. Thomas planted plane and locust trees.

SMALL, PROFESSOR WILLIAM. Small, who numbered among his friends some of the most intelligent men in England, returned there in 1766. He died before the Revolution.

TUCKAHOE. The house, now privately owned, still stands on the James River near Richmond.

WILLIAMSBURG. The capitol of Virginia until 1779 was in the heart of the busy Tidewater plantation area. But as more people moved into the mountains and the Piedmont area, the little town was not close enough to the state's growing population centers. After the capitol moved to Richmond, Williamsburg ceased to grow. By 1927, many old houses had been torn down and replaced by "modern stores and gas stations." In the 1930s John D. Rockefeller, Jr. became interested in restoring the old city before *all* its colonial homes disappeared. Today you can walk through its streets and see it just as it was when Peter and Tom Jefferson knew it.

WYTHE, GEORGE. Tom's teacher of law was a well-known lawyer and judge. He became the first law professor at the College of William and Mary and was a patriot of the Revolution. He helped draft the Virginia Constitution and the Constitution of the United States. Wythe was murdered by his nephew, but he lived long enough to ask Thomas Jefferson to make sure the nephew did not inherit his money. You can visit the Wythe House at Williamsburg and see it just as Tom Jefferson did when he was a young law student.

Thomas Jefferson: The Man

1767   Became a lawyer and was admitted to the bar in Williamsburg

1769   Was elected to the House of Burgesses as the representative from Albemarle County

1772   Married Martha Wayles Skelton, a young widow

1774   Wrote "A Summary View of the Rights of British America"

1775   Wrote a Reply to Lord North and was a delegate from Virginia to the Second Continental Congress

1776   Wrote the Declaration of Independence, dated July 4, 1776; in September, went back to the Virginia legislature, where he began getting rid of the old feudal system imposed on Virginia by British tradition

1779   Was elected Governor of Virginia, the year that the state capitol was moved from Williamsburg to Richmond

1780   Was re-elected for another year as Governor

1781   Returned to his home at Monticello in June

1782   Worked on a natural history of North America called *Notes on the State of Virginia*; became a widower on September 6

1783   Was elected to the first Congress of the new United States, where he introduced our decimal system of coinage

1784   Was sent as a representative to Europe to make commerce treaties so the new United States could trade with other countries

1785   Became Minister to France; in Virginia, his bill to establish religious freedom was adopted

1789   Returned to the United States in November

1790–   Served as Secretary of State under President George
1793   Washington

1796   Was nominated for the U.S. presidency but John Adams, with three more votes, became President and Jefferson became Vice-President

1797   Became president of the American Philosophical Society in Philadelphia, Pennsylvania, the first group to begin making scientific and historical collections of the New World's natural science and history

1801   Became the third President of the United States; published *A Manual of Parliamentary Practice*

1803   Doubled the size of the United States with the Louisiana Purchase

1804   Sent an expedition to the West led by his Piedmont neighbors, Lewis and Clark

1806   Sent the Pike Expedition to explore the Rockies

1809   Returned once more to Monticello

1814   Sold his collection of 10,000 old and rare books to the U.S. Congress to replace those burned by the British during the War of 1812

1825   Saw the beginning of another of his dreams, a college in the Piedmont region, when the University of Virginia opened

1826   Died on July 4 at Monticello at age eighty-three, on the fiftieth anniversary of his Declaration of Independence

Author's Note

Libraries, librarians, and the interlibrary loan system are a historical author's best friends. Among those helping with this book were, in Virginia, Albemarle County Historical Society Library, Charlottesville; Alderman Library, University of Virginia at Charlottesville; Colonial Williamsburg Foundation Library at Williamsburg; Swem Library, College of William and Mary, Williamsburg; and in Pennsylvania, Free Library of Philadelphia; Historical Society of Pennsylvania Library, Philadelphia; Jenkintown Library, Jenkintown; The Library Company, Philadelphia.

Index